After the Wedding

After the Wedding

A Guide for the Bride
by Sharon Collins

PRAIRIE **MOON** PUBLISHERS

TULSA, OKLAHOMA

Prairie Moon Publishing
Tulsa, Oklahoma
© 1990 Prairie Moon Publishing. All rights reserved.
ISBN 0-9627526-0-6
Library of Congress Catalogue Number 90-92065

Manufactured in the United States of America

Book and cover design by Carl Brune.

Illustrations by Heidi Priddy.

Cover photograph by Rick Stiller Photoworks.

Photograph of Sharon Collins by Lackey Photography.

This book was printed on sixty-pound Cougar Natural Vellum by
Walsworth Publishing Company, Marceline, Missouri.

The typeface is Caslon Old Face No. 2 and Nuptial set by
ProType, Inc. of Tulsa, Oklahoma.

Introduction

The Piano Player and the Barber

An Overview of Marriage

The Piano Player: Listening to My Own Music

The Woman in Marriage

Who Keeps the Castle?

Maintaining the Household

. . . But Can She Cook?

Cooking Skills

The Caterers Can't Always Come

Entertaining

Index

Acknowledgments

First acknowledgment must go to my husband, Ed, who encouraged me to pursue my ambition of sharing this book, and believed wholeheartedly in its purpose.

A special thanks to Anne Thomas for her diligent work of editing and proofreading the manuscript with a keen eye and wise counsel.

Many thanks to Freemount Marketing of Tulsa for their expertise and guidance in presenting a book to the public, but most of all for their contagious enthusiasm.

Much gratitude to my mother-in-law, Eunice, who created foods so tasty as to inspire the development of my own culinary skills and endeavors.

Appreciation to my neighbors, Ralph and Pat Thomas, for their generosity in providing a typewriter for the first manuscripts.

Finally, I acknowledge the support of my entire family and friends whose attitudes of love and encouragement gave me endless strength and joy.

Introduction

*M*any days have passed since I was a new bride, and I am still excited and inspired about marriage. I know the value of a strong husband-and-wife relationship; I know the joy of sharing your innermost self with the one you love and admire.

As a new bride, all I knew for certain was that I was very much in love with my husband, Ed! I had few, if any, skills in homemaking, and I knew even less about dealing with a marriage relationship.

Now, after more than 30 years of marriage, I am delighted to share with you some of the things that have worked best for me in creating both a home and a relationship. In the pages that follow, I touch upon many areas that now affect your married life. I include recommendations and tips for managing your home, principles and ideals to strengthen your marriage, and personal incidents and examples from my own marriage.

I am a musician and a homemaker, not a writer, but this book has evolved from my love and respect for marriage — the bonding, the friendship, the warmth, and the affection between two people who have joined their lives together. It is my deepest desire that After the Wedding *will encourage and guide you to develop your marital relationship into a strong, everlasting, and joyous one.*

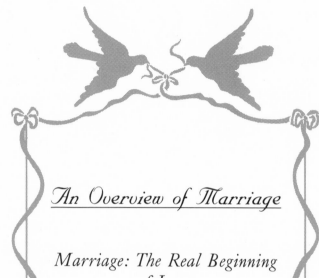

An Overview of Marriage

Marriage: The Real Beginning
of Love

Two Lives ~ United

The Male Personality

After 11,315 days of growing together, Ed and I are still making music, cutting hair, and enjoying the choice we made years ago — that of choosing each other.

After a day of helping children make music from those black and white bars we call piano keys, I pause and sigh with thankfulness because I know that soon I'll see Ed coming home, with other people's hair still clinging to his shirt and wearing that boyish grin that won my heart over three decades ago.

What a combination we are — a piano player and a barber — and within our world of music and hair, we have managed to raise three children and go through a paralyzing accident from which Ed is almost totally recovered.

I feel blessed when I consider my world and the people who fill it. The thoughts of our love, and the respect that we have for one another, cause my mind to travel back to the years when Ed and I first began to build our universe. Those years, and even the first hours after we said "I do," make me realize that although we had watched many couples move to the music of matrimony, most new brides, myself included, proceed without a musical score. There's little doubt in my mind that the life the piano player and the barber enjoy today is the result of an earlier commitment to see our worlds become one universe; big enough for both our dreams yet special enough to protect our love.

I am not a professional counselor — I'm just a happy piano player who fell in love with the barber. And this is my gift — the music score, if you will, to you, the new bride. I would like to share with you life after the wedding; those memorable and exciting first days.

Marriage ~ The Real Beginning of Love

As you begin a new life as a mate and lifetime partner, your actions and attitudes already are setting the pattern that will affect your marriage for years to come. As hard as it may be to realize now, you alone will become a great impact on your marriage and your husband.

Keep in mind that first and foremost, marriage requires *commitment*. You already began this process when you took the marriage vows; they were a pledge of the present as well as the future. How you handle this commitment can only be seen through the test of time and duration. We live in a society today that seems to find it more and more difficult to come to terms with commitment. We fear the failure, pain, disappointment, and hurt that can result from making permanent decisions. Granted, these things sometimes take place in a commitment, but there are always the joys, the warmth, the rewards, and the peace that are returned to you for having remained loyal to your vows.

The world in which we live is certainly an imperfect one, and we must realize that fact; we must expect to have times of distress and difficulty, for they will surely come. However, I think you will find that the happy and good times will far outweigh the stormy ones.

You can develop several qualities within your character that can help you immensely in becoming a stronger wife. First of all, make up your mind to be *consistent*. I am reminded of the scripture that "God is the same yesterday, today, and forever." What a model for us to follow! Can we be by our loved one's side daily through all circumstances? Will we be there when it is great fun, or even the reverse? Being consistent will bring, in time, the trust so necessary

4

for a good marriage. It will mean being steadfast, firm, and having continuity free from variation. This cannot be practiced only when you feel like it, but must become a part of your daily life. Giving your best today is the best recipe for a better tomorrow.

Another characteristic much needed in marriage is that of being *authentic*. Don't be afraid to show who you really are. Being yourself is the greatest asset you can have. God designed you as a special individual and your "real" self has much more to offer the world than any imaginary one. So take pride in yourself, focus in on the wonder of creation, and look toward your strong points as well as accepting your frailties. It is all a part of being human, and humankind is a very beautiful thing, indeed.

Another trait to acquire for a closer bond in your relationship is that of *unselfishness*. Learn to put others first with a spirit of generosity. Seek out ways to give to others; the dividends you will receive can be astonishing. You will grow more in this area the more you use it. Remember that true joy can be found only in developing unselfish attitudes.

Finally, then, consider attaining *tirelessness*. Do not tire of the challenge of your goal for a life shared together. Continue to be enthusiastic. It does sometimes take great effort, but the effort is not in vain. Give your best in terms of strength and energy. In doing so, you will be making an investment in your marriage and your mate. Then, do not anticipate instant success. There is no such thing.

Two Lives ~ United

$\mathcal{M}$olding two lives together — lives consisting of unique individuals from separate backgrounds — can be an enormous task. No couple is completely united when the marriage ceremony is performed; their real union is the work of the years that follow. Although the union is a gradual process, there is nothing to compare with the fruits of your labor in creating this bond.

I am reminded of a friend and neighbor, Bonnie, who called me recently about taking piano lessons. (I have been teaching piano since I received my music degree in 1966.) Bonnie's husband Bill had just given her a piano and she was most anxious to learn to play, as it had been a life-long dream. It was also a very opportune time to study the piano because her children were now grown and Bill had retired.

One day, at Bonnie's piano lesson, she shared with me about the wonderful times she and Bill have been having since his retirement. They do everything together now, and have become the closest of friends. They spend real "quality" time with one another. Previously, they had devoted many years to rearing four children. During most of that time, Bill had traveled frequently in his business, which had put extra responsibility and strain on Bonnie. Naturally, there were times when she had wondered if the effort of holding the family together was even worth it. (You see, the tedium of life gets to all of us!) But her testimony to me that day was memorable and touching. Tears welled up in her eyes as she admitted that she easily could have missed out on this beautiful time with her husband. Had she not endured the rough periods during their marriage, she never would have known the closeness she and Bill share today. She had had no idea that life could be as heavenly for them as it has become. You should see them! They enjoy all things together. They take walks, work in the yard, enjoy frequent trips, and build a relationship with their grandchildren. They are a delightful and inspiring couple.

So you see, for marriage to work and survive the inevitable difficult times, you must first of all desire unfailingly that it work. Strive for a good marriage — but do not expect a perfect one. Determine within yourself that it can last and endure, knowing that in the current world this is becoming increasingly more difficult. Decide to do whatever you have to do to keep your marriage afloat, without making any assessment of what's fair. Fairness is not the issue, the issue is sacrificial love. Such love must become the basis of your marriage. You may find yourself many times having to walk the extra mile; so be willing to do so. If you enter marriage for what you can get from it, you'll never gain true satisfaction. But if you enter the covenant with a determination to give the best you have, unselfishly, you will find the greatest of fulfillments.

~ *Faith* ~

One underlying thought that has meant a great deal to me when marital distress came, was to remind myself that Christ wants the very best for us. Christ sanctions marriage, and He desires that our marriages be fulfilling, vital, fruitful, and long lasting. Therefore, when circumstances stand in the way of that fulfillment, I am strengthened when I recall that it is *not* God's will. I must carry on by showing patience and allowing time for a remedy to take place. It can be a real test of faith, but it gives great satisfaction and internal peace because I know that I am helping to protect something in which God participates. I must emphasize that if I did not have this belief, I could not withstand the storms when they come, and would easily doubt the potential success of marriage. The scripture from 1 Corinthians 13:4-7 is appropriate: "Love is patient and kind; love is not jealous or boastful; it is not arrogant or rude. Love does not insist on its own way; it is not irritable or resentful; it does not rejoice at wrong, but rejoices in the right. Love bears all things, believes all things, hopes all things, endures all things."

~ *Perspective* ~

At the very outset of your life together, expect both happy and sad times. Valleys will come as well as the mountain tops; marriages are *not* fairy tales made from storybooks. In fact, true love is full of many beginnings. The first years usually are the most difficult, as you both are making many adjustments in sharing your lives together. Be careful not to hang your whole well-being on the juggling of marital emotions. Often the most petty things stand in the way of marital harmony. This is quite normal, but as time goes by, you will gain more expertise in either dealing with these obstacles or simply overlooking them. It becomes a matter of perspective. *I think I spent about half of my first year of marriage crying. My feelings were easily hurt; I took everything personally. Then one day it dawned on me what a baby I was; it was simply time to grab hold of myself and grow up. From then on I was able to walk a straighter path toward marital maturity.*

So continue on, keeping in mind that a special relationship between a man and a woman deserves your very best effort. Take seriously your wedding covenant. Learn to forgive and rebuild trust as many times as is necessary. You may have to do this numerous times through the years. But marriage is never more than what you put into it. Study to advance the happiness of each other. Attend marriage enrichment seminars, read books on obtaining healthy marriages, and observe couples who have had strong and satisfying relationships in marriage.

~ *Trust* ~

There are many essential ingredients for creating a harmonious marriage. One of the most important, in my view, is *perfect confidence*. I have seen the lack of this literally disintegrate a marriage. Perfect confidence produces the trust mentioned earlier in this chapter. You must work diligently to build a strong sense of trust in one another; trust must be earned and takes time to develop.

But each passing day can deepen its roots. Strive never to betray the confidence your mate has entrusted in you. There are many things that belong only to the marriage circle. Retain and protect that privacy with all your heart. I think this is easier to do if you do not live too near family or close friends. Often, it is much too easy to tell personal problems and concerns to them. The temptation to put your private marital life "on the street," so to speak, can dilute the magic of your bond. Keep your marriage sacred and refrain from discussing your intimate world with outsiders. It is no one else's business what goes on within your marital relationship. Much discipline may be required of you in order for you to achieve this, but believe me, it will pay many dividends.

Allow me to emphasize the importance of trust and confidence by giving you the following example. Let's say you have had a serious disagreement with your husband. He became angry and said things to you that hurt terribly. Naturally, you were quite shaken by this, and during a luncheon date with your mother, the issue came up. You shared a detailed and emotional account of the event; you had never felt worse in your life. Later that day, however, you and your husband are able to work out the differences; you both forgive one another and seal it with a kiss. You are able to put old feelings behind you and carry on as before. But, your mother is not in on the "forgiveness and make-up" session. She is left worrying over you; the next time she sees your mate, she still will have ill feelings for the way he treated her daughter. You see, you have painted a negative picture of him. Also, if your husband is aware of these confidences having been made public, he might feel uncomfortable around your family. It is a "no win" situation. You must not fall into such a trap.

~ *Individuality* ~

Another aspect of marriage that merits mentioning is that of respecting your companion as an individual. As close as the marriage union is, we are still individuals and need to be treated as such. Do not attempt to read your mate's mind or assume to know everything he thinks, wants, or likes. Be sensitive to your husband's opinions and preferences. Ask him frequently about his views so that you can gain more insight to his needs. *This was one of the hardest lessons for me to learn. As a new bride, very much in love, I assumed that how I felt, he felt also; that what appealed to me would naturally appeal to him, too.*

Now let me take this one step further and give a word of caution on dealing with your spouse's individuality. The greatest temptation both parties get into is that of trying to change one another. I did not see the nature of this problem for years, and I must stress the severity of this tendency. There is no quicker way to destroy your mate's confidence in himself than by revealing your negative or corrective views of his conduct, behavior, and personality. Your role as a wife does not make you responsible for what he *is* or *does*. You are responsible only for yourself and your own actions.

Something about being married seems to make us feel that we own our mates. This "ownership policy" causes a wide range of problems; it is probably the root of most marital horrors. There are no perfect human beings, yet we expect our mates to be so. Put the criticisms and nit-picking behind you before they grow completely out of proportion. Be kind, patient, and encouraging. Seek to discover your mate's attributes rather than his defects. Enjoy the traits that attracted you to your husband to start with; then accept and love him for the person he is. In doing so, you will allow him to continue growing and maturing into a wonderful companion.

~ *Communication* ~

We cannot continue looking at marriage without mentioning communication! Communication is the key factor in creating a healthy marriage. It is vital to a relationship, and offers a great means of expression. Learning to talk things out together is invaluable. It can also be the most fun. *My husband Ed and I have spent countless hours in our backyard swing sharing intimately with one another. It is our haven in the world of perplexity; it is our time daily to renew our closeness, rekindle our affection, and keep abreast of each other's needs. We get so much from the beauty of the earth; it is quiet, the sunrise is gorgeous, and most importantly, we are alone that few minutes before we begin each day. We watch the birds feed; we see the changes in nature as we meditate together. Having a time and place to touch base daily with one another is essential to our spirits.*

Mornings may not be your most convenient time; you may prefer a late evening walk or a chat on the porch after dinner, but *all* couples need time to be a couple. They must have moments to communicate regularly. Begin a system of this sort now, and you will grow closer than you ever could imagine. Your house will become a home, and your relationship will become a more joyous one. Be an innovator, striving in any way possible to become closer and more as one. What better satisfaction can there be? It has been said many times, "There is nothing as priceless as a good marriage." When you observe a couple with a strong marriage, you will see two people who have learned the importance of communicating.

~ Goals and Future Plans ~

As the two of you spend more time in conversation, include a time of planning for the future and looking ahead. Talk out your dreams and goals; settle on some common ones to shoot for as a couple. Be careful not to set unrealistic goals that carry unattainable expectations. Keep in mind also that many of our aspirations are influenced by the society we live in. They may not be the right choices for your own way of life. They may not be feasible goals for you as a couple, or goals that would give you any satisfaction. For example, I have seen couples strive for material wealth to the point of being consumed by it. Allow your finances and material possessions to come about gradually, in due time. Do not expect to have everything from the start; the price you pay for these things may be far too costly to you in more ways than the dollar figure.

Consider also the value of love, joy, peace of mind, good health, leisure time, and serenity. Together, search for the needs that are meaningful to you as a couple, and make sacrifices only for the things you consider worthy. Then, as you accomplish each goal, by all means take time to celebrate; give yourselves a pat on the back for a job well done! *Unfortunately, Ed and I have neglected to do so. Looking back over the years, when a car loan or land purchase was paid in full, we failed to recognize our accomplishment. We are more aware of that today, and are trying to do better by stepping aside momentarily to acknowledge our achievements. I trust that you will learn to do so early in your marriage. You certainly deserve an applause at those appropriate times!*

As I review my 30 years of married life, I empathize with newlyweds. When we marry, there is a dramatic change in our lives, and it occurs almost instantly. In addition, there is very little preparation for each of us as we enter this "new world" of matrimony. No wonder that at times it can be overwhelming. But we must press forward, giving our best, and rising to the occasion at hand, hoping for the kind of union that God desires for us. After all, hope is our greatest commodity; we must always hold onto it.

The Male Personality

For years, I have heard men complain about the problems of understanding women. That works both ways; husbands, likewise, are difficult for wives to understand. But you need to attempt to unravel some of these mysteries in order to become a better wife.

Over a period of time, I have made some observations concerning the male personality. Of course, not all things I have observed will apply to all men at all times. But, by the same token, I think there are some fairly universal points worth considering.

You must come to terms with the fact that men and women are not the same creatures. Putting aside the obvious physical differences, there are still numerous other differences, both psychological and emotional. What should you know about these wonderful creatures that are so masculine, appealing, good looking, warm, cuddly, cute, protective, witty, adorable, strong, helpless, interesting, and endless other descriptions?

~ The Male Ego ~

First and foremost, you must accept the fact that men have enormous egos — egos with an insatiable need to be fed. Begin early to develop a great sensitivity to fulfilling this need. In so doing, you will reap many benefits indirectly, because men thrive on encouragement and attentiveness. (But please, do this honestly, and with sincerity.) Your husband should always *be* number one, and *feel* that he is number one, above anything or anyone else, including your closest friend or even your parents. He must be fully convinced that your love for him is dearer to you than anything else on this earth. Be perceptive to your mate's physical, emotional, and spiritual desires. Do not allow your husband to become an island, and encourage him to talk frequently and share his inner feelings. Too often, men fear that by revealing their feelings, they will appear weak and unmasculine. As you continue to give your mate your undivided attention, he will grow to confide in you. Also, teach your husband to verbalize his feelings and compliments for you. Many times, men feel that the fact that they are a faithful mate speaks for itself in displaying their love and admiration for you. But you need to hear those accolades and may need to lead your husband into telling them to you.

Constantly encourage your husband in his work. Repeatedly tell him how much you appreciate it, and frequently inquire about his work day. Wives can be the craftsmen of the marriage, molding and shaping the relationship. If you are a working wife, walk carefully here. Acknowledge that working wives often intimidate the male. A husband's feeling of importance may diminish, and he may somehow feel unneeded. So, continue to reinforce his importance to you; let him know how much you depend on him. Strive to turn off your work when you are with him. This is difficult and may seem totally unfair, especially when you have many business concerns of your own buzzing in your mind. Nevertheless, make an effort to talk less about your job. Then, endeavor to make your moments together quality time, away from the intrusions of the outside world. *I had a chance to put this practice to work after Ed and I had been married several years. I suddenly had the opportunity to attend college to acquire a much-desired degree in music. Ed agreed and shared this goal for me. But, deep within, I recognized it could be a hardship on him emotionally. Therefore, the first day that I attended classes, I made a pact with myself not to study or talk college during our usual family time. I would have supper ready when he arrived home, as I had done previously, and would try to remain low-key. This was not easy, but I felt it was worth a try. As badly as I wanted to continue my education, it was not worth the risk of losing my marriage. As closely as I could, I maintained our way of life according to the routine we had become accustomed to, hoping my husband would not feel threatened by my new goals. We continued having our evening time together; I learned to utilize every free moment between classes by studying in the library on campus.*

Now if I had additional work left to do, I would slip out of bed very early, at whatever time I felt necessary to complete my assignments. Thus, Ed did not feel excluded from my life because of college. I have never regretted being sensitive to this matter; the extra care and precautions were well worth the energy spent.

~ Being Supportive ~

Be careful not to take your husband for granted. Compliment him every chance you get; if you fail to do so, he may look elsewhere for reassurance. I heard Zsa Zsa Gabor once say, "Husbands are like fires. They go out if unattended." Your mate constantly requires your attention and approval, although he may not realize it himself. The biggest targets for infidelity are the men with the greatest insecurities. A man's need to be assured and uplifted can transform the affections of others into dangerous temptations that too often lead to affairs. In general, I think men are basically insecure, which is all the more reason to keep a check on their emotional well-being. If you feel you are married to an exceptionally insecure man, you may have to take even more care to build him up; underscore his importance to you, and point out his strong traits and accomplishments. He should have your unqualified acceptance; it is the first step in making your man come alive. If you cannot meet this challenge and fill this void, your husband ultimately will find someone who will. Believe me, there are many women ready and willing to tell him the things he wants to hear; it might as well be you, his spouse and lover. After all, you have a lifetime of matrimony to protect! *On a television show recently, I heard a prostitute being interviewed. She remarked that her clients desire companionship, and someone who is a good listener, as much as they desire the sex act. Could there be a lesson there for us, as wives?*

Of course, men aren't the only people with insecurities. Be careful that you do not suffocate your mate; he can't use that much affection. Be certain that you are not compensating for your own lack of assurance when you demand too much attention. Some women carry this trait from childhood without even realizing it. Possibly they were starved for affection in some way, and later expect their mate to

15

make up for that void. Make sure your husband has some time and freedom of his own. Every person deserves this consideration. *As a new bride, I had this lesson to learn. Ed and his dad had a family tradition of bird hunting during each fall season. First of all, I had not grown up around sportsmen, and secondly, I couldn't imagine that he would want to go hunting when he could spend that time with me. I took it personally, and behaved like a spoiled child. I could not view it any other way until later, when I had matured enough to see the difference.*

As we continue to consider ways to become better wives, try helping your husband to grow in confidence by instilling leadership qualities in him. It is important for him to "fill" and "feel" his role. Frequently ask your husband his opinions concerning certain matters. Let him know you *value* his wisdom, enlightenment, and ideas. Develop a habit of seeking the solutions he may have for daily problems. Be sure that he sees how much you appreciate his talents, resources, and contributions. He should sense that you need him and depend on him. Allow him to take charge of the family, and to be responsible to God for it. In that way, he can continue to grow into the mature and stable person that you will enjoy in years to come.

~ Affection and Attention ~

This can be accomplished as you spend time with your husband. As discussed earlier, you should set aside your own "together times," which can be the most fun of all and can really tap your creative resources. Plan a picnic after work in a nearby park, or surprise him with a lunch basket of food to share, or simply get on the phone and call him for a date. Be spontaneous; keep monotony from setting in by showing frequent impulses of affection. *Not long ago, my sister-in-law even sent flowers to my brother's office on his birthday. Why, you never saw anyone so thrilled! Men like receiving flowers, too.*

I am reminded of another occasion that illustrates just how much men love affection and attention. About two years ago, I became a volunteer in a women's organization for helping children with physical and mental impairments. One of their most effective fund-raisers was held on Valentine's Day. For a twenty-five dollar donation, a person could send his or her sweetheart a singing valentine. We, the volunteers, were dressed in darling red, pink, and white costumes with a large heart on them. After we sang, "Let Me Call You Sweetheart," we handed the recipient a box of candy with a signed valentine from the sender. We traveled in pairs and were given destination sheets that had us scheduled to sing for someone every fifteen minutes, which really kept us hopping! Of course, the assignments were arranged in the same general vicinity, but it still required real coordination in getting to each appointment. We sang for doctors, schoolteachers, yardmen, businessmen, and others. The responses were wonderful; grown men showed every kind of reaction from embarrassment to joy. I'm sure it was a day that they will not soon forget. They were truly surprised and impressed.

~ *Being Positive* ~

You see, men love being around cheerfulness and positive thinking. Take care to be a happy and cheerful person yourself, refraining from getting caught up in a whining syndrome. A negative and dissatisfied attitude is one of the quickest ways to discourage your mate. Eventually he will lose respect for you, and more than that, will probably choose to be around others who offer happier conditions. Don't sell yourself short; don't take life too seriously all of the time; don't forget how to laugh; and develop a good sense of humor. Maintain a positive outlook on life with a zest for living, and your husband will appreciate you and long for your company and companionship. Consequently, you will become his best friend as well as his lover.

Take care, too, to protect your man's self image. Uphold his image in public, always! Do not tear him apart in front of others, even jokingly. He really needs to be tops in your eyes and desires that the public see this in you also. If you criticize him in front of others, it will deprive him of his manhood. If you see weaknesses, do not emphasize them. Keep in mind that men reach maturity later than women do. Therefore, in some instances you may need to carry the ball for awhile. *My mother, who raised two sons, always contended that boys had to reach about thirty years of age before they really began to grow up. It is an interesting theory. I have seen that be the case in several instances. I had a friend once who became so despondent over her husband's immaturity, that after years of investment in their lives together, she consented to a divorce. Not long afterwards, her ex-husband finally reached a mature status. However, his new wife reaped the benefit of his previous wife's investment, and my friend cheated herself of the dividends she had earned. She had almost completed the task of seeing him through the formative years, and just when he was nearly through it, she gave up. Of course, this would not happen in every case, but do be careful.*

~ Physical Communication ~

Communication, as was mentioned earlier, is of utmost importance in keeping a relationship healthy and happy. But another form of communication in marriage is that of sexual enrichment. You must exercise patience here, because we each come from different backgrounds with various expectations of sexual satisfaction. For instance, let's say you come from roots that prohibited premarital sex. Now, suddenly, sex is acceptable and expected. How can you immediately turn on a green light where there had always been a red one before? Or, let's say you have different ideas of sex than your mate does. Both of these things take time to work out, so give them time.

You must continue to communicate with one another in order to come to a common ground. Some men do not intuitively know how to satisfy a woman sexually. You may have to guide your husband to behave sexually in a manner that is pleasing to you. Also, what is termed "normal sexual behavior" can vary widely. Decisions about whether an activity is right or wrong rest with the couple. Simply share with your partner what you like or do not like, and come to an agreement or compromise on the subject.

Sexually, males are more easily aroused than females. Men are extremely sensitive to sexual cues and stimuli. Women, on the other hand, seem to relate more to loving gestures and a feeling of being loved, protected, and respected. Women also enjoy caring and loving phrases, warm embraces, and tender kisses. Do not assume your husband already knows this. You may be the one who will need to encourage him to do so. On the other hand, there may be times when sexual fulfillment can be of utmost importance to the man, almost to the point of desperation. Although you may not share such a degree of sexual urgency yourself, try to develop an acceptance and understanding of the male's greater need to express himself sexually. Even when your passion is not as great as his, you can be warm and responsive. Do not make him feel "weird" or abnormal. There may be incidents when you don't particularly desire to make love, but you can do so because of your love for your spouse. Love him whenever you can, but if you must refuse, be gentle and kind.

Some women find themselves craving to make love when their husbands do not desire it. Be careful not to make your husband feel guilty or inadequate. Remind yourself of his delicate ego, and his strong need to be manly. Don't give him the impression that he has, in any way, let you down or disappointed you. At times, worry, stress, or fatigue can inhibit sexual activity. Be patient; in a lifetime of marriage there will be plenty of opportunities for lovemaking. Be certain your husband is *totally* convinced that you are satisfied and happy with him as your lover. Sexual intercourse is an act of love; treat it as such. Touch your husband all you can. Our basic need in life is to be touched, loved, and comforted. Reassure him that he is very desirable to you; he wants you to enjoy lovemaking as much as he does. Look into his eyes, and really see him; admire his body, too. During the sex act, learn to concentrate on the moment and block out the rest of the world. Sexual expression between two people who love each other very much can be one of God's greatest and most satisfying gifts. Treasure it with all of your heart; protect it, nurture it, guard it from the world. And most of all, remain true to one another. That way, you will never lose the joy intended for a husband and wife. When you surrender your life to your husband, you become beautiful to him. Proverbs 31:10-12 says it well. "A good wife who can find? She is far more precious than jewels. The heart of her husband trusts in her, and he will have no lack of gain. She does him good, and not harm, all the days of her life."

The Piano Player: Listening to My Own Music

The Woman in Marriage

Woman's Unique Value

Staying Attractive ~
Keeping Fit

Physiological Insights

We farm wheat in Nowata County, Oklahoma. We entertain continuously. I love the feel of the dirt as I garden, and I thank God for the warmth of life He has given. I have cooked for hundreds; I have nursed my husband back to health. I have taxied my children all over creation, and, surprisingly, I have taken care of me.

Before I was a wife, mother, and then a grandmother, I was a woman. I was filled with dreams and ambitions. I was proud of my unique body, and even more plesaed that Ed had singled me out to be his music for the rest of his life. And being his music means being his woman.

We have spent many moonlit nights together, and I'm still impressed with the barber, and likewise, he with me. But I am a woman — unique and special — and it gives me great pleasure to invite you to set aside what you are doing so that I can share with you the knowledge I wish someone had shared with me. Don't be embarrassed; as I said earlier, I'm not a professional — I'm just a piano player sharing her music with you.

Woman's Unique Value

I admire women; they have a vast amount of strength and goodness to offer. I have observed them display the qualities of encouragement, persistence, faithfulness, endurance, vision, love, patience, wisdom, and many other assets. I have seen women hold families together; I have seen them serve unselfishly in schools, hospitals, churches, and neighborhoods with an unending spirit of giving. I have seen them adjust to unavoidable changes in their lives, and handle the situation beautifully. There are many whom I admire greatly, and I certainly acknowledge their worth as they serve with fervor through various channels; I hope they are aware of their contribution to the world. However, it is unfortunate that many women do not give themselves due credit; they fail to see their value.

Where does your worth lie? Do you feel you have any real value? You may be astonished that I would raise such a question, but the number one problem among women today is that of "low self-esteem." Can you believe that, in this modern world? Even our society has done itself a great injustice not by recognizing the full value of womanhood. As a result, many women feel unimportant — even apologetic about themselves. Sadly, some even marry expecting it to be the answer for a blissful life. If that is your reasoning, you may be in for a startling surprise; you already may be heading for great disappointment. Others are not responsible for your happiness so much as *you* are responsible for it. Actually, happiness comes from within. How, then, can you learn to acquire this inner peace usually called happiness?

~ Role Models ~

First, I believe we need *role models*. It is imperative that you have at least one woman whose qualities you really admire; someone who can be an inspiration for you; someone you identify with who can be a springboard for your development as a woman. I am sure there are important women in your life who have had an influence on you. Take advantage of your own role models. Observe them; learn from them. Allow the experience of their lives to touch your own life.

I have been fortunate to have had several wonderful role models. They have meant a great deal to my life and I would like to share their qualities with you. They have taught me much, by example, and have remained special to me for many years. One of them is my Aunt Lorraine, my father's sister, and a very loving and gentle woman. When I was a child, I watched her every move. How impressed I was with her warmth, vitality, and creativity! She demonstrated this especially through her cooking. For example, Aunt Lorraine would come occasionally to visit our family on the farm where we lived, and upon arising early in the mornings, would make the roundest, prettiest, tastiest biscuits you ever put in your mouth. (Maybe that is why I love to cook!) She was fun, optimistic, and refreshing to be around. Since reaching adulthood, I have visited her home numerous times and it has always been a treat. Her home reflects her inner beauty. She makes everyone feel special, and she is a most gracious hostess. In addition, she raises a vegetable garden, then cans her produce and also creates wonderful jellies and jams. But most of all, she makes you feel worthy. I never reflect about special people without having my Aunt Lorraine come vividly to mind.

Another role model for me, but in a much different way, has been my mother. In my earlier years, I didn't recognize this fact so much, but as I have grown older I have seen it more and more. My mother was never really as much a homemaker as a professional person. However, she displayed a zest and vitality for life that few ever really experience. Her energies have always remained unlimited, and her enthusiasm stimulating and contagious. She was a pioneer of sorts, holding job positions that

25

previously had been occupied only by men. For example, she was the first woman draftsman hired by a major oil company, and later in life became a physician at a time when women doctors were a rarity. My mother is an optimist, a dreamer, and a hard worker, and above all, has a great compassion for people. She always sees the best in them, and always is ready to give them the benefit of the doubt. What a gifted person for me to have known and grown up around!

Still another strong influence in my life is a very good friend who attends the same church that I do. The very first time I met Ginger, I remember saying to my husband Ed, "This lady can't be for real. No one is really this nice!" But twenty years of knowing her have certainly proven my first impression drastically in error. Ginger has a way with people; she genuinely loves them. In fact, I have heard her mention friends' names with such endearment that you might assume they were her closest relatives. She shows genuine concern for their well-being through her many gestures of kindness. She even has the special ability to remember the individual, personal trials and triumphs of their lives. In addition, Ginger runs her home like a well-oiled machine, giving attention to all the details a comfortable, loving home requires. She is a marvelous entertainer who has the skill to quietly and effortlessly transform a small dinner party into a much larger one at a moment's notice. Last, but not least, Ginger is a loving wife, mother, and grandmother; she is treasured greatly by her family.

Once you have role models in mind, see to it that you are around them enough to continue to benefit and grow from them. Then continue to build in yourself confidence and self-esteem. Do not isolate yourself or become an island; grow as an *individual,* even within your marriage. In doing so, you cannot help but become more valuable and fascinating to your spouse. Of course, keep your priorities always in order. Next are suggestions that will make a difference in your life:

~ Be Joyful ~

Believe in yourself; be authentic and real. Be tender, compassionate, and gentle, with the capacity to love and care for others. You can literally "wear" these qualities. Make it a habit to look for the beauty in the world. Create a positive environment wherever you can. Listen to good music; open the drapes and let the sunlight in. Love people; do a good deed for someone. Good deeds are a blessing "twice," benefiting both the receiver and the giver. Praise God daily for your blessings, and when negative thoughts surface, quickly replace them with positive ones. *For example, when my husband tracks in mud from the yard, I remind myself how sweet he looked earlier that day as he made the bed to surprise me before he left for work.*

~ Love Yourself ~

Learn to love yourself as God loves you. (We usually have been taught to do everything *except* to love ourselves.) This is not egocentric self-love, but confessional self-love. Practice thinking of positive words that best describe you; even write them down as you think of them. You may have difficulty with this at first, but as you begin to practice it, it will become easier. Think of words like: friendly, cheerful, trustworthy, patient, alert, intelligent, energetic, humorous, and many more.

~ Be Creative ~

Develop ways to express yourself through your creativity. You can do this through various channels. Try several out; you will eventually find the one right for you. The ability to create will become a very meaningful part of your life. It will also keep you "alive" and interesting. Consider the following list, and build on it:

cooking, painting, gardening, designing, decorating, acting, writing, sewing, entertaining, and playing music.

Of course, there are many, many more, but by developing interests of your own you not only become a more radiant individual, you also avoid hanging your whole sense of well-being on the influx of marital emotions. Life has much more to offer when you are doing something you really enjoy, and you are not likely to be bored. Use your creativity to avoid a cycle of self-pity, which could mushroom into a large obstacle for you. Refrain from harboring ill feelings; they take a toll on your own well-being. Our responses to life determine ninety percent of the quality of life we experience. View life as a challenge, not a threat. Then learn to live one day at a time.

~ *Be Content* ~

Contentment is probably one of the most difficult attitudes to acquire. We live in a very progressive, competitive society, but we need to recognize the difference between healthy aims and unhealthy ones. Learn to be content with each stage of life; grow where you are planted. Each era has its own rewards. Also, you will avoid much stress and strain by not allowing yourself to place too much emphasis on material possessions. Besides, a wife who behaves in a nagging, dissatisfied way will turn her husband and others against desiring her company. A thought I saw once in a magazine has since helped me to keep a perspective on this matter: Happiness is not having what one wants, but wanting what one has.

Staying Attractive ~ Keeping Fit

We have touched on the vital importance of a woman's inner beauty and strength, but let's not overlook the necessity of maintaining an outward glow. Admittedly, it is easy to get comfortable in marriage, and after a while to lose sight of your physical appeal. You may also become so absorbed with the demands of daily life that you fail to give your appearance top priority. I have seen evidence of this when I go to public places and see young wives and mothers who simply have "let themselves go." They give the impression that once they "got their man," they quit running the race. In reality, the race is beginning on the day of the wedding!

I once knew a girl who continuously had a weight problem. Upon reaching adulthood, she dieted and lost all of her excess weight, and looked great. Soon after, she met a young man, fell in love, and later married him. Unfortunately, she has not been trim since. I often wonder if her husband is still searching for that slender girl he married.

I admit that the husband may be just as guilty as the wife by being complacent about his appearance, but two wrongs don't make a right. Let's remember, though, that one of a woman's greatest virtues is her inspiration and encouragement. Few things inspire a man more than an attractive, well-trimmed companion in life. Get in touch with your physical body as well as your inner one. You need both, working together, to make you a complete woman. This doesn't mean you need to be a fashion-model type, but it does mean that you need to make the most of what you can be. That's all anyone should expect, and it is not an unreasonable expectation.

Actually, good grooming merely shows others that you care for and respect yourself, and that is the first step toward caring for others. Now that you are married, however, you probably already have noticed that you have a great deal less time for yourself. It's much more difficult to take care of your grooming needs. Therefore, you may need to make some changes in your dress, and reset your priorities according to the time you now have. You may need a simpler, easier-to-care-for hairdo, and a simpler mode of dress that can enable you to get ready and out the door much more quickly. Consider coordinating clothes with fabrics that are easier to care for and hold up longer. If you think about streamlining your grooming habits, you can come up with a good look that requires much less time to maintain.

Begin your life together by making it a habit to check your appearance each day, 10 to 15 minutes before you expect your husband home. Such simple things as brushing your hair or putting on fresh lipstick can make a difference. Always prepare for his homecoming; after all, he is your man and is the most important person in your life. Strive to remain attractive to him always. Greet him radiantly; make him feel happy to be with you. Keep your relationship fresh and exciting. At times this may require a tremendous effort, but I guarantee that it will strengthen your relationship and help it grow into a long-lasting one.

Another point to consider is to make your bedroom a special place that the two of you share together. At times, add fresh flowers, candles, or soft music and lights. Use your imagination. Keep a variety of nightwear, too. You wouldn't dream of serving the same menu every night for dinner; by the same token, don't get into a rut of wearing the same favorite robe or gown. Be versatile, be exciting, and stay interesting.

~ *Exercise* ~

Then, if you haven't already done so, get on some kind of an exercise maintenance program. *Anything* beats *nothing!* It is very tempting to live a sedentary life, but through the exercise, you will not only feel better, you will look better, too. Here are some extra tips:

1. When doing your housework, bend from your waist when picking up things from the floor. You will have touched your toes numerous times by the time you have finished your cleaning.

2. When you are shopping, never look for the closest parking space. Deliberately park far enough away that you will be forced to walk more in your daily routine.

3. As you talk on the phone, remain standing and go up and down on your toes. This exercises the calves.

4. Anytime you are walking, whether it be shopping or running errands, get in the habit of moving more briskly, holding your back straight and maintaining good posture. Not only will you look better, you will burn extra calories, as well.

At one time in my life, I felt that I had lost my energy, and each day I would drag through my usual routine. It never seemed to improve, and I became quite concerned. Finally, I picked up an article about a young mother of three toddlers. She was having an awful time keeping up her energy to care for the little ones, day in and day out. One night, her husband arrived home from work and suggested that she get out of the house, away from everyone. She began walking each evening when he returned; eventually her walking turned into running. She was delighted to find that this time to herself, combined with the invigorating exercise, gave her abundant energy. Suddenly, she was able to breeze through the days with her children, and eagerly to anticipate her run in the evenings. Later she became one of the top women runners in her community. However, my eyes were glued to the words "more energy" in the article, so I decided to give it a try. Bear in mind that I am a person who never had a trace of athletic ability or sports background.

Initially, I started out the door and ran a few blocks, then walked a few, ran some more, walked some more; finally one day, I could run an entire mile! I was so excited and pleased with myself that I called Ed at work to announce my triumph. Since that time, I have increased my distance, but most of all, I am happy to report that the energy I needed also returned. You actually have more energy when you return from a run than you had before you set out. I share this experience because if I could achieve this, anyone can!

If you decide to try running or jogging, it is critical to purchase the proper shoes. Start out slowly, with short distances. Some additional tips on running are:

1. Consult your doctor before starting a vigorous exercise program.

2. Eat and rest properly every day.

3. Run three or four days a week, with one or two days in between for rest.

4. If you cannot carry on a conversation while running, you should slow down, and enjoy your run.

5. Always stretch before and after your run.

If you are trying to lose weight, run when you are slightly hungry. When you return, you will feel less hungry. Running also provides a great time to meditate. You have no interruptions, and you are alone with your own thoughts. You can run and at the same time plan the evening meal, pray for a friend, listen to the birds, plan a dinner party, observe the flowers and trees, or simply enjoy the fresh air in your face. For me, running is both refreshing and exhilarating.

Certainly, jogging or running is not for everyone, but find the form of exercise that is best for you, and do it. Whatever form of exercise you choose, I encourage you to include some kind of outdoor activity, so that you can take in this great world in which we live. In my neighborhood, a group of women meet every morning and walk three or four miles together. (I read an article recently by a physician who stated that brisk walking burns more fat per mile than jogging.) Walking or jogging is referred to as an aerobic exercise. Other aerobic exercises include such activities as bicycling, swimming, and rope-jumping. These exercises should be vigorous enough, last long enough, and be done regularly enough to keep the heart and lungs in good shape. To achieve the cardiovascular benefits of aerobic exercise, you should exercise 20 to 30 minutes at a time, at least three times a week. By doing so, you will experience many rewards:

- firm, lean body
- strong heart and lungs
- lower blood pressure
- slower heart rate
- muscle strength and endurance
- energy and enthusiasm
- self-confidence
- self-discipline

Finally, stay sexy! Of course exercise will play an important role in accomplishing this, but sexiness comes also from within, from being sure of yourself and feeling comfortable with yourself. Let's review the highlights:

1. Remember that you have a body that needs exercise.

2. Dress in a manner that shows off your best features tastefully.

3. Be yourself; don't try to be like someone else.

4. Wear things your husband likes, such as his favorite color or style.

5. Maintain good grooming habits.

6. Be a true companion to your husband.

Physiological Insights

$\mathcal{G}$ood health contributes greatly to a happy marriage. It is important to know the essentials about your body. Not terribly long ago, such awareness was not so accessible. During the Victorian era, in the latter part of the 19th century, a woman could not have her body examined by a male doctor, and she had to indicate on a drawing where her pain was. Even in more recent times, the sexual taboo was so great that women often were not very familiar with their physical functions.

Today, women can be much more open about their bodies and their sexual roles. With increased knowledge and more open attitudes, women's health care and hygiene have received benefits unheard of even a generation ago. Your reproductive self is so intricate and priceless that it certainly pays to know it well so that you can care for it properly. Gynecologists sometimes remark that the more they study the intricacy of the female reproductive system, the more awed and admiring they become. As a young woman, if you develop a sensible regimen of care for yourself it not only will bring you beneficial results now, but it will also determine how you look, act, and feel in your later years. An intelligent and informed approach to health maintenance will contribute to your continued vitality. You will be able to shape a better and more fruitful life for yourself and those closest to you.

To help you maintain good general health, consider the following guidelines:

1. Refrain from smoking cigarettes and limit your use of alcoholic beverages.

2. Be moderate in using medications such as laxatives, sleeping pills, and pain relievers.

3. Eat properly; include foods from the four food groups: milk, meats, vegetables and fruits, and breads and cereals.

4. Establish a sensible and regular exercise program.

5. Develop good sleep habits; rise and retire at approximately the same times daily.

6. Maintain good bowel and bladder habits; drink plenty of water.

7. Strive to develop good posture; it improves blood circulation and helps prevent muscle strain.

Then, be sure to carefully choose a doctor that you can be comfortable with and can communicate with. If and when health problems occur, you will already be established with a physician in whom you have confidence.

~ *Gynecologic Exam* ~

All sexually active women should have a full gynecologic examination once a year. Some dread the exam and fail to take proper care of themselves. Any minor unpleasantness from an exam, however, is far outweighed by the benefits of disease prevention and early detection. Every woman should make regular screening part of her health program, since cervical smears and breast exams are crucial to early detection of disease and early detection is critical to successful treatment. Despite the current trend toward fitness and well-being, many women still do not take enough care of their bodies.

A full gynecological examination begins with recording your medical history. It is helpful if you can give details of previous tests and problems, dates of your last few periods, and any other facts or complaints you may think relevant, including your method of contraception.

The doctor will examine your breasts with the purpose of detecting abnormalities that may be early signs of breast cancer. A pelvic exam will then be carried out to reveal any signs of disease, abnormal growths, or damage or infection in the uterus, cervix, or vagina. A cervical smear (Pap smear) is routine with all gynecologic examinations. The procedure is painless and entails lightly scraping off some of the cells of the lining of the cervix (neck of the uterus) with a wooden spatula. The sample is then sent to a laboratory to be examined. After the gynecologic exam, do not forget to ask any questions you may have; it is helpful to make a list before you arrive.

All women should get into a habit of examining their own breasts every month. It is important to know your body; then you can identify any abnormal changes in your breasts.

The best time to examine your breasts is immediately following your period, for sometimes the breasts are more tender and lumpy just prior to menstruation.

Signs to watch for are:

- unusual increase in the size of one breast

- a lump, or lumpy areas, in the breast

- one breast unusually lower than the other

- puckering of the breast skin

- nipple of one breast turning inward

- fluid emerging from one breast only

- a rash on the nipple

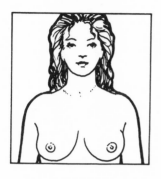

1. Sit in front of the mirror stripped to the waist. Sit completely straight, then carefully study your breasts. Look for any marked change in size and see if one breast has recently become lower than the other.

2. Examine the nipple. Has it drawn back or turned in since your last examination? Inspect the inside of your bra for any signs of discharge. Look at the skin of the breast for any puckering, dimpling, rashes or changes in texture. Lift the breasts to examine them underneath. Raise your hands above your head and see if there is any swelling or skin puckering on the upper breast or around the armpit.

3. Lower your arms and raise them to chin level. Have both nipples moved upward to the same extent? Lean forward and examine each breast for unusual changes in outline, dimpling or retraction of the nipple.

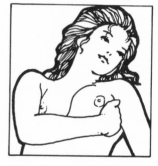

4. Lie down in a relaxed, comfortable position, either on a bed, with your head on a pillow and a folded towel under your left shoulder blade, or in the bath. Put your left hand under your head. Examine your left breast with your right hand. Use the front part of the flat of your hand and keep your fingers straight and close together.

5. Slide your hand above and below the nipple, from the armpit to the center of the body. Press gently to feel for lumps.

6. Pass your hand from the bottom of the breast, across the nipple and upward to the armpit. Slide your hand sideways and diagonally across the breast and over the nipple, making sure you have felt all parts of the breast. Feel for any lumps in the armpit or the top of the collarbone. Now examine the right breast with your left hand.

~ *Birth Control* ~

Since sexual fulfillment is such a vital part of marriage, you, as a couple, have the responsibility of choosing a birth control method that best fits your circumstances. In doing this, consider how important preventing pregnancy is to you, and how suitable a particular method might be for your needs. With so many options available today, you can probably find at least one type of contraceptive to satisfactorily fit your lifestyle. Although each type of contraceptive is accompanied by a degree of risk or failure, keep in mind that most of them work safely most of the time.

Be aware of the misconceptions and falsehoods concerning the chance of conceiving if you do not use contraceptives. Some people are quite misinformed and believe that a pregnancy will not occur:

- without full penetration of the vagina by the penis,

- if the penis is withdrawn before ejaculation,

- if the woman does not experience orgasm,

- if the woman is a breast-feeding mother, or

- if the woman immediately follows sex with douching.

Without the use of contraceptives, a woman *can* become pregnant, in spite of the above circumstances. It is always better to be safe. Together, plan your method of prevention, and lessen your risk of an unplanned pregnancy. Later, then, when conception is desired, you will be able to plan it at an appropriate time.

~ *Method of Contraception* ~

THE CONDOM

What Is It?	a sheath of thin rubber that fits over the erect penis
How Does It Work?	catches the semen, which contains the sperm, and prevents it from entering the vagina
How Reliable Is It?	97 - 98%
What Are The Advantages?	easy to use and attain convenient to carry use when needed allows the man to be responsible may help men prevent premature climax
What Are The Disadvantages?	must be put on during lovemaking when the penis is erect can cause men to feel less sexual sensitivity spermicide used with condoms may irritate penis or vagina may slip off or tear
What Else Should Be Considered?	must never be reused lubricate with a jelly

THE PILL

What Is It?	pills that contain synthetic hormones, similar to the estrogen and progesterone produced by a woman's body
How Does It Work?	prevents the ovaries from releasing an egg each month
How Reliable Is It?	98 - 99%
What Are The Advantages?	simple, convenient, easy to use, doesn't interfere with lovemaking reduces bleeding and cramps with periods reduces risk of anemia regularizes periods
What Are The Disadvantages?	must be taken regularly (daily) & completely may cause weight change may cause water retention may cause high blood pressure may cause nausea, moodiness, headaches may cause sore breasts increases risk of vaginal infections

What Else Should Be Considered?	not recommended for women with a family history of diabetes
	not recommended for women who have had blood clots or inflammation of the veins
	make it a practice to have regular exams

DIAPHRAGM — WITH SPERMICIDE

What Is It?	a saucer-shaped device of rubber or rubber and plastic (must be used with spermicidal cream or jelly)
How Does It Work?	inserted in the vagina so that it covers the cervix (the opening of the uterus); sperm cannot enter the womb
How Reliable Is It?	97 - 98%
What Are The Advantages?	can be inserted 2-3 hours before intercourse
	no side effects; use only if needed
	can be part of bedtime routine
What Are The Disadvantages?	may inhibit lovemaking; creams and jellies are messy, and more must be added if intercourse occurs more than 2-3 hours after insertion
	creams can irritate penis or vagina
	can cause bladder infection for some women

What Else Should Be Considered?	not recommended for women who dislike touching their genitals
	must be fitted by a physician
	should be left in place 6-8 hours after intercourse, then washed, dried, and stored in a cool place
	check for small holes or weak spots
	renew every year or with 10-pound or more weight gain
	not recommended for women with sagging uterus or uterus that has poor muscle tone

INTRAUTERINE DEVICE (IUD)

What Is It?	a device of plastic or copper placed inside the uterus
How Does It Work?	uncertain — may stop fertilized egg from implanting in the womb; brings about changes in the lining of the womb in a way that discourages pregnancy
How Reliable Is It?	95 - 98%
What Are The Advantages?	always in place
	doesn't inhibit lovemaking

What Are The Disadvantages?	may cause increased bleeding and cramping during periods partner may be able to feel the string attached to the IUD during intercourse may cause backaches may cause pelvic infections
What Else Should Be Considered?	can puncture the womb increases the chance of tubal pregnancy; not recommended for women with a history of tubal pregnancies insertion usually done during menstruation because the opening of the cervix is softer

RHYTHM AND FERTILITY-AWARENESS METHOD

What Is It?	a method of using the calendar, body temperature, and amount of vaginal mucus to determine when chance of pregnancy is greatest

How Does It Work?	requires the discipline of keeping a daily chart of the woman's physical signs; body temperature drops slightly just before ovulation, then rises when the egg is released. Cervical mucus also shows changes around ovulation time. Backache and depression are sometimes other signs of ovulation. The calendar is used to work out the pattern of menstrual cycles. All of this information works together to help a woman discover the days each month that an egg is likely to be released
How Reliable Is It?	76 - 80%
What Are The Advantages?	no side effects; no medication allows intercourse without contraceptive partners share responsibility acceptable to most religious groups

What Are The Disadvantages?	must keep accurate records every day
	sexual frustration; no sex during fertile
	    time (unless couple chooses to use
	    a contraceptive)

What Else Should Be Considered?	illness or lack of sleep can produce false
	    temperature signals
	not reliable if woman's menstrual periods
	    are not regular

THE SPONGE

What Is It?	a small, soft sponge
How Does It Work?	fits inside vagina, over the cervix to block and absorb sperm; contains chemicals that kill sperm
How Reliable Is It?	89 - 92%
What Are The Advantages?	use only when needed; easy to use can purchase in drugstore can be inserted several hours before lovemaking, and left there as long as 24 hours
What Are The Disadvantages?	may increase vaginitis; may irritate the penis or vagina can be difficult to remove; sponge can tear can make intercourse dry

Foams, Suppositories, Creams and Jellies

What Are They?	substances made with sperm-killing chemicals

How Reliable Are They?	80 - 90%

What Are The Advantages?	no side effects can purchase at drugstore; easy to carry and use use only when needed

---

What Are The Disadvantages?	must be put in vagina not more than 20 minutes before intercourse can be messy and can leak may irritate the vagina or penis more must be inserted if intercourse is repeated

~ *The Human Reproduction System* ~

Both sexes have organs that produce and contain reproductive cells. These organs are called the gonads.

The gonads of the male are the two testes, or testicles. They are located in a pouch of skin called the scrotum. In the scrotum, the testes are maintained at a temperature of a few degrees below the normal body temperature. This lower temperature is essential for the production of viable sperm. The testes produce a hormone, testosterone, which controls the development of secondary sex characteristics, such as a deep voice and facial fair. Another important function of the testes is to produce sperm cells, or sperm.

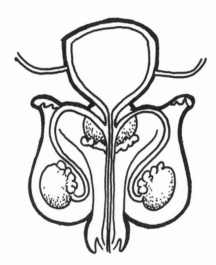

MALE REPRODUCTIVE ORGANS

Within the testes are about 500 tightly coiled tubes called the seminiferous tubules. Cells within the seminiferous tubules divide and form sperm cells. As the sperm are produced, they then pass to a storage area called the epididymus. When sexual excitation takes place, the arteries supplying blood to the penis of the male dilate. Blood accumulates in sinuses, or chambers, in the penis, which becomes erect and rigid and is able to penetrate the vagina of the female. Further sexual excitation results in ejaculation. Sperm then pass from the storage area into the vas deferens. Contractions of the smooth muscles of the wall of the vas deferens propel the sperm forward. Glandular secretions are added to the sperm by the seminal vesicles, the prostate gland, and Cowper's glands. These secretions probably serve to activate the sperm, and constitute the fertilizing fluid called semen. Semen provides the sperm with food for energy and the proper environment for survival.

The human sperm cell (also called a gamete) is very small compared with the human ovum, which is the egg produced by the female. The male gamete is a small, active cell. It obtains its energy from the semen, which has a high concentration of fructose (sugar). It takes as many as 130,000,000 sperm cells to insure the fertilization of one ovum.

The gonads of the female are called ovaries. These ovaries contain about 400,000 ova, or eggs, but only 300 to 400 are released during the female's reproductive years. The two ovaries are near, but not connected directly to, the oviducts, or Fallopian tubes, which are lined with cilia, or hairlike fibers that move rather like grass in the wind. When an ovum is released from one of the ovaries, the action of the cilia draws the ovum into the tube. Then the ovum moves down the Fallopian tube to the uterus, or womb. The uterus is a hollow, muscular organ with thick walls. It is lined with a mucous membrane containing many small glands and capillaries.

The released ovum dies and disintegrates if it is not fertilized. Then it is discharged through the narrow neck of the uterus, called the cervix. The cervix opens to the vagina.

The development of the ovum preparing to be released is coordinated with a monthly buildup of the lining of the uterus. This is controlled by hormones. Human ovaries usually produce only one

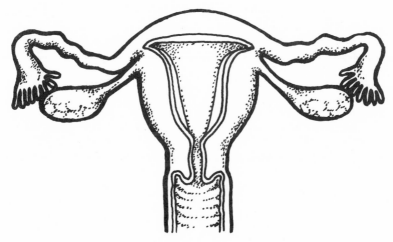

FEMALE REPRODUCTIVE ORGANS

egg in the course of a 28-day cycle of activity. The cycle begins with the release of a hormone produced in the pituitary gland. This hormone is called the follicle-stimulating hormone (FSH). FSH causes a mass of ovarian cells to form a follicle in which the ovum matures. As the ovum matures, the follicle fills with fluid that contains the hormone estrogen. Estrogen is responsible for the secondary sexual characteristics of the female, such as development of the breasts and broadening of the hips. The pituitary gland senses the estrogen that diffuses into the blood, which stops the pituitary from producing FSH.

When the ovum is mature, the follicle breaks through the wall of the ovary and the ovum escapes. This is called ovulation. The ovum is picked up by the Fallopian tube nearby. The follicle is now called the corpus luteum. This development is controlled by another hormone from the pituitary gland, called the luteinizing hormone, or LH. LH is produced as a response of the pituitary to estrogen in the blood. The corpus luteum now secretes the hormone progesterone. Progesterone maintains the growth of the mucous lining of the uterus. If the ovum is not fertilized, the corpus luteum degenerates, and no more progesterone is produced. The lining inside the uterus detaches and sloughs off. The breakdown and discharge of the soft uterine tissues and the unfertilized egg is called menstruation.

The uterine cycle has four distinct stages:

1. menstruation, which averages about five days;

2. the follicle stage, from the end of menstruation to the release of the ovum, which averages 10 to 15 days;

3. ovulation, the release of a mature ovum, which occurs at 10 to 14 days after the first day of the cycle (day 1 of menstruation); and

4. the corpus luteum stage, from ovulation to menstruation, which lasts 10 to 14 days.

~ *Common Gynecological Infections* ~

The female genital tract is warm, dark, moist, rich in glands and blood vessels, and bathed in a number of secretions. It is profoundly susceptible to infections. In fact, few women escape having some form of infection (inflammation and irritation of the vaginal tissues) at some time during their life.

Vaginitis, a broad term for any vaginal inflammation, can damage one's personal well-being. It can itch or burn, and often produces a foul-smelling discharge quite different from the normal vaginal secretions.

Vaginal discharge is not always caused by an infectious agent, however. Pregnancy, the use of oral contraceptives, or just the cyclic surge of estrogen preceding the menstrual period, can cause heavier-than-usual secretions from the vagina. Chemically caused vaginitis can result from excessive douching, perfumed toilet tissue, bubble bath, or vaginal sprays.

Let us consider one of the most widespread forms of vaginitis due to infection: trichomoniasis. It affects both men and women. In women, trichomoniasis causes excessive discharge that is usually foul smelling, and an itchy or burning sensation. It is terribly bothersome. In the male, this disease can lurk with no symptoms at all or can cause a slight burning during urination. Males, therefore, can be unknown carriers of the disease. So, if you get a "trich" infection, it's essential for both you and your spouse to be treated.

Trichomoniasis has been responsible for countless marital break-ups. The woman sees her doctor for a "trich" infection. Her husband probably has no symptoms and thinks she has been cheating on him. In reality, the *Trichomonas* organism can probably stay dormant in the body for many years. It can be harbored not only in the vagina and in the male genital tract, but also in the urinary and intestinal tracts of both men and women.

The second most common problemmatic cause of vaginal discharge is Candidiasis, often referred to as a "yeast infection." Candidal vaginitis can be acquired by sexual contact, but it can also result from self-infection from stool or contact with contaminated objects. The symptoms can be quite disturbing. Tissues of the labia and vulva (female's external genitals) may become very red and swollen. Vaginal tissues may bear yellow or white patches and produce an irritating discharge. Itching can be severe, especially at night, and urinating or sexual intercourse can cause painful burning. Again, men can have *Candida* infections without showing symptoms.

Good general hygiene may help you avoid candidal infections. A lifelong rule for girls and women is always to use toilet tissue from front to back when wiping. This will help you avoid contaminating the vagina with traces of stools. Since yeast thrives in a warm, damp environment, women should avoid airtight crotches in underwear. Instead, wear absorbent cotton underwear and cotton-crotch panty-hose. Also, avoid sitting around in a wet bathing suit in the summertime. Sometimes, a change of diet is helpful if you are continuously bothered with yeast infections. Sugar encourages the growth of yeast; this is why diabetics are frequently troubled with yeast infections. Reduce your intake of sweets, alcohol, and sugary foods that raise blood sugar levels. When you must take antibiotics, eat plain yogurt and insert a small amount directly into the vagina at bedtime to help restore your body's bacterial balance. Certain oral drugs, and vaginal creams such as Monistat, can help eliminate yeast infections. Stronger antifungal medications can be prescribed for very stubborn cases. However, before running to the gynecologist with vaginal itching, try these simple cures:

> Take a salt-water bath. Dissolve one-half cup of table salt in tub. This saline solution works to clean the vaginal area much like tears clean your eyes.

> Try a vinegar sitz bath: To a few inches of warm water, add one-half cup of white vinegar. Then sit with your feet propped up on the sides of the tub so that the water rushes in.

Do not try frequent douching for relief of any vaginitis. Over-douching can itself cause vaginitis through drying and shrinking the vaginal tissues.

Another type of vaginitis is referred to as Honeymoon Cystitis. It got its name because of its prevalence at times of high sexual activity, and because the mechanics of intercourse can force infective material up the urinary canal toward the bladder. Symptoms are pain and burning while urinating or during intercourse, with a hot sensation climbing up the urinary canal. Therefore, cystitis is an infection of the bladder. It is easily treatable, usually with sulfa and antibiotic medications. The problem is that cystitis can return repeatedly in some women. Simple preventive measures can help you avoid urinary tract infections:

1. Empty the bladder before and promptly after intercourse.

2. During the day, empty the bladder regularly.

3. Drink generous amounts of water.

~ *Menstrual Cramps* ~

Magnesium plays a role in regulating female hormones and is also a natural diuretic. If you have problems with cramps, boost your daily magnesium intake by eating lima beans, kidney beans, wheat germ, whole wheat, and nuts.

Also, vitamin E relieves cramps because it increases circulation and gets more oxygen-carrying blood to the uterus.

Exercise also is helpful in easing cramps. Anything that exercises the major muscle groups, gets you to breathing hard, and massages the pelvic area, is beneficial. Examples are jogging, swimming, cycling, and fast walking.

In addition, heat can soothe the pain by relaxing the uterine muscles and increasing bloodflow.

Women's menstrual periods vary enormously, even in the length of the monthly cycle, but the average loss of blood is only about two ounces. Irregular, painful or heavy periods are not unusual, especially before having babies, but should not be tolerated unquestioningly. A proper diagnosis should always be made by your doctor. Even the worst symptoms of menstrual problems can be alleviated through self-help or medical treatment.

A special thanks to my mother, Dr. Harriett C. Sherrill, D.O., for her assistance and consultation in compiling the information of this chapter, Physiological Insights.

For additional information regarding your specific medical needs, see your personal physician.

Who
Keeps the
Castle?

Maintaining the Household

A Wholesome Home

Housecleaning Help

Laundry Tips

Organizing Time

Money Management

A piano player and a barber who were teaching piano and cutting hair in the '60s certainly could not afford a castle! But wherever love lives, whether in an apartment, a condo, or a cute little bungalow, it can make your home a castle fit for your lives together.

I laughed when I started writing this, because three decades ago most household responsibilities would have fallen to the wife. Today, however, sharing is becoming a wonderful part of the marriage union.

But for you, the new bride, I have some helpful secrets for maintaining the household. Be quick to share some of these with your husband. Encourage him to help you "keep the music going." After all, it is the continuation of daily tedium that creates an atmosphere that nurtures your love, and allows it to flourish forever.

A Wholesome Home

Being in charge of your own home is much like having your own company or enterprise. In essense, you are running your own business or corporation. You have the unique position of providing a haven, or an oasis, hidden away from the outside world of demands and enormous pressures. A well-maintained, love-nurtured home environment can be the mainstay of the family. Strive to develop a warm and attractive home with a pleasant and inviting atmosphere. It should be a place where cheerfulness, courtesy, and love abide; the mood of your home is set primarily by you. You have the power to lift it to the highest realm, or bring it down to nothing. What a responsibility, but what an opportunity!

A wife wears her home much in the same manner that she wears an article of clothing. It is a reflection of her; it is the way she chooses to present herself to the outer world. The course of action you choose for caring for your home displays the importance you place upon it. I truly believe that the people who get the most out of their homes are the ones who put the most into them, not necessarily in terms of money, but in effort. It may be your first home, but it can be everything you want it to be.

It has been said that "cleanliness is next to godliness." That may be a bit exaggerated, but there is a lesson here to be learned. I'm sure that anyone can appreciate a well-organized and comfortable home. However, time does not always allow this possibility. In such cases, learn to "top clean." My neighbor calls it "cleaning in the round" — going around catching the most obvious spots. So, at the least, make the bed, clear the dishes, empty trash, and pick up the clutter. This kind of cleaning doesn't take long, but certainly helps your general attitude and outlook; usually it is not dirt that bothers us as much as messiness and disorganization. (I have made it a habit to spread up my bed the moment my feet hit the floor. This seems to always get my day immediately underway.)

I never knew the meaning and importance of good housecleaning until I got to know Mrs. Lola Giblin. While I was finishing up my work at the university to complete my degree, Mrs. Giblin kept our two young children in our home. In addition to babysitting, she did light housework and laundry. She was a jewel; she could clean like no one else I had ever seen. She had a knack for restoring new life to things in my home that I had given up on — things I thought needed replacing. She had a clever way of making "old things" look new again. I even had given up on an old toaster that didn't work any longer; Mrs. Giblin ingeniusly took it apart and repaired it.

But, most of all, Mrs. Giblin knew the meaning of making the best of what you have. She taught me, probably unknowingly, two valuable lessons:

1. Take care of what you have, and it will serve you a long time.

2. With a little determination, almost anything can be kept like new.

You see, it makes little difference whether you live in a modest home or a luxuriant one. If you do not learn to take care of it, no home can give you real satisfaction.

I am reminded of a time when I was looking for a home to purchase in our area. The real-estate agent spent an entire afternoon showing me home after home that he thought might fill the bill. That experience was some time ago now, but I still remember how amazed I was to see homes with a very attractive outside appearance turn into utter disappointment for me once I got inside them, because they were so unkept and neglected.

Keep in mind that few people love housework, but nearly everybody appreciates a neat and enjoyable home. Thank you, Mrs. Giblin, wherever you are. I always loved coming home on the days you were there:

Imagine, though, how different it is for us to keep house today compared with the pioneer women just two or three generations ago. They didn't have modern detergents, automatic washing machines, or electric ranges, and certainly no microwaves. Think about cooking on a wood-fired stove, or even over a fireplace. Laundry was done outside, weather permiting, in large black kettles heated with firewood, or even in the creeks. Clothes were scrubbed vigorously on washboards and many women made their own soap. Clothes were hung to dry on clotheslines, for there were no automatic dryers, and supermarket was not a word in their vocabulary. Most food was raised on the premises, and much hard work went into planting and reaping it. Can you picture what your home would be like without all the many conveniences we know today?

My neighbor, Bonnie, shared a neat story with me that portrays the many changes that have taken place in our households in a relatively short period of time. She tells it this way:

"At the age of 92, Bill's grandmother visited us for the first time in our new home in Tulsa, Oklahoma. The year was 1966 and the home was a 'Gold Medallion' which meant it had all of the latest appliances and conveniences.
She had not been to Tulsa since the railroad had gone through at the turn of the century, when she had lived in a tent in Sapulpa (a town near Tulsa). At that time, Sapulpa was larger in population than Tulsa. Her first child was born in a tent in Henryetta, Oklahoma. So you see, she truly had been a pioneer woman with none of the luxuries that we now know.

"She was fascinated with our new home — the gas starter in the fireplace, the central air- conditioning, the garbage disposal and other modern items.

"After having been here for two days and watching me in my daily routine of putting laundry in an automatic washer, then into an automatic dryer, I hastily loaded the automatic dishwasher and turned it on. She very nonchalantly looked up at me and asked, 'What machine is that you've got working for you now, honey?' "

~ *Housecleaning Helps* ~

*The following household cleaning hints may be beneficial to you
as you become a homemaker.*

- As much as possible, put your household duties on some type of routine.

- Keep a memo pad in the bathroom for your shopping list.

- Combs, curlers, and brushes can be cleaned by soaking them in water to which baking soda and bleach have been added.

- Clean the toilet bowl by sprinkling with baking soda and adding vinegar; if you are going to be gone a few days, add a little bleach to toilet bowl to whiten it.

- To clean ceramic tile, use a mixture of $\frac{1}{8}$ cup vinegar to $\frac{1}{2}$ gallon of water.

- Clean glass shower doors with a cloth dampened in white vinegar.

- Alcohol removes scum from bathroom fixtures.

- Spray the shower with a 50:50 mixture of liquid bleach and water; spray weekly to discourage mildew growth.

- To open clogged drains, try pouring one cup salt and one cup baking soda down the drain followed by boiling water.

- To remove water rings and stains from inside glass, dampen the inside and add any toilet bowl cleaner; allow to stand 10 minutes.

- Formica stains can be removed by using a paste of baking soda and water; let stand a few minutes before scrubbing.

- Oven spills can be lifted by soaking a cloth in ammonia; leave on the burned area for awhile, then scrape away the residue.

- Oven spills should be sprinkled with salt immediately.

- Pour baking soda on kitchen grease fires to extinguish flames.

- Ink stains sometimes can be removed with hair spray.

- Chandelier pendants can be cleaned by dipping them in a container of one part alcohol and three parts water; place a drop cloth underneath the chandelier and allow to drip-dry.

- Avoid leaving your home while appliances are operating.

- Small scratches in glass table-tops can be removed with toothpaste.

- When doing housework, save steps by keeping cleaning supplies in a basket that can be carried from room to room.

- Shaving cream will clean upholstery.

- Wax the bottom of chair legs to prevent scratching of wood floors.

- Make cleaning ceilings and corners easier by placing an old sock over the end of a yardstick; secure with a rubber band.

- Brighten carpet by sprinkling with cornstarch; let stand and then vacuum.

- For pet stains on the carpet, pour club soda straight from the bottle; then blot with a dry towel.

- Place a piece of charcoal in your tool box to absorb moisture and keep tools rust-free.

- Camphor gum helps keep mice away; it can be purchased at hardware and garden stores.

- When purchasing items, keep original boxes and packaging; they will be easier to store away, will stack better, and will remain protected, too.

- Burned pans can be cleaned by sprinkling heavily with baking soda; add water to moisten and let stand several hours.

- To clean copper pots, rub with Worcestershire sauce.

- Club soda cleans and polishes kitchen appliances.

~ *Laundry Tips* ~

I hardly think of laundry without thinking of Jim Beller, a pleasant and amusing fellow who sings in our church choir. I always remember him referring to the "magic drawers" that existed in his bedroom when he was a boy growing up. He explained that no matter when he opened these drawers, they always contained clean and neatly folded socks, underwear, shirts, and jeans. It didn't even depend upon which moment he chose to look in them; magic-magic, the clean clothes were always there.

Then, one day, when he left home to go to college, something very earth-shattering occurred. The magic drawers were no longer working. He wondered what could have happened, and why there were no clean clothes in them. Reality had hit, and what a shock!

Sometimes, I think that is the way a new bride must feel. Suddenly, the responsibility of clean clothes and doing laundry is a major task in a life that already has many new territories to conquer.

In the years to come, you too will be amazed at the amount of time you will spend doing laundry. But, a pretty laundry is a wonderful thing, so learn to do it to the best of your ability.

- Before laundering, sort clothes, screen for stains, and always check contents of pockets.

- Use hot wash water and bleach for white clothes (nonsynthetic), and rinse in hot water.

- Use warm water for colored clothes and synthetics; rinse in cool water.

- Fill washer with water and detergent first; then add clothes gradually, making sure agitator moves freely — do not overload.

- Improper rinsing is the main cause of graying in clothes.

- Use a timer for your washer; clothes left there will sour.

- Use a timer for your dryer so that you can remove clothes the minute they are dry; this eliminates excessive wrinkling and wear on fabric fibers.

- Too much soap causes graying in clothes; use a little less than product calls for.

- Cut fabric softener sheets in half; a full sheet is not necessary to do the job.

- For general stains, try a sudsy solution of Tide™; also a product called Shout™ is helpful.

- To get white cotton socks really white again, boil in water to which a slice of lemon has been added.

- Never soak clothes longer than 10 minutes; the dirt will cling to the clothes again.

- Equal parts of turpentine and ammonia will remove paint from clothes.

- Wash new sheets, towels, and table napkins before using; it softens the sheets and napkins, and removes lint from towels.

- Save on costly energy bills by placing heavy items such as bath towels and jeans outside to dry; when they are nearly dry, tumble in the dryer to fluff.

- Avoid using dryer during peak high-use hours.

- Keep lint screen on dryer clean at all times.

- Occasionally give your washer and dryer a good cleaning; it will make doing laundry seem more enjoyable.

- White vinegar will remove old hem creases; apply, then iron.

- To retain whiteness, store white linens in blue tissue paper.

- Hang a small cloth bag of dried lemon peelings in your closet to discourage moths.

- Never use clorine bleach on nylon or polyester; instead use Rit Fabric Whitener and Brightener™

- Synthetic fabrics should always be dried on "low;" fabric softener stains may occur if a small load is dried at the higher setting

- To cut down on pilling of sweaters, synthetic fabrics, sheets and quilts, line-dry them to prevent the rubbing that causes pilling.

- Matching garments should be laundered the same amount of times to avoid a difference in shade of color.

STAIN REMOVER GUIDE

Blood If you act quickly, bloodstains can be removed with hydrogen peroxide.

Chocolate Soak stain in cold water, then work in detergent; Launder in water as hot as is safe for fabric.

Grass Stains First, check for colorfastness, then try applying rubbing alcohol, and flush with cold water. You may need a few drops of ammonia.

Grease Immediately rub dishwashing liquid (Dawn™) on the spot, then launder as usual.

Gum Harden with ice, then scrape gum off with a dull knife, rinse and launder.

Hair Color Spatters can be removed from towels and clothing by using Tilex™

Ink Stains Squirt cheap hair spray directly on the spot, then rub with a clean cloth; or try full-strength alcohol.

Lipstick Rub first with toothpaste, then launder.

Makeup Rub shampoo or Dawn™ dishwashing liquid into the stain; or try hair spray, let stand 30 minutes, then launder.

Mildew Soak clothing overnight in a large bucket of water with two cups Clorox™ bleach and one-half cup Borax™ added.

Mustard	You must work quickly; rinse well, then spot clean with Fels Naptha™ bar soap (Or use glycerine). If stain remains, try rubbing alcohol.
Perspiration Marks	Flush with white sudsy ammonia or try vinegar. On a collar, remove the ring with an old toothbrush and a cheap shampoo.
Shoe Polish	Remove stain from colored fabrics with one part rubbing alcohol and two parts water. On white fabrics, use the rubbing alcohol full strength.
Wine	Immediately saturate with club soda, then wash as usual.

NOTE:

1. When using a stain remover, always test garment first in an inconspicious place.

2. Do not combine chlorine products with ones containing ammonia or acid; it could cause hazardous gases.

~ *Organizing Time* ~

*O*rganization is the key to attaining much success in your life, whether it be with personal objectives or professional ones. I have always used lists to help me keep abreast of obligations, needs, and commitments. I find that if I do not write these things down, they may never get completed. You may want to employ such a method also, because at a glance, you can readily see your course of action. However, you should write your projects down in the order of their importance. Begin your day with number one; stay with it until it is finished. Then, start to work on number two, and work until you reach the bottom of the list. If you don't get through the entire list, you at least will have completed the most important items. Developing the habit of doing this daily will bring you wonderful results, but always prioritize each item. You will discover that you can accomplish much more in a day than you ever thought possible. However, keep in mind that there is never enough time to do everything but there is always enough time to do the most important things.

On your list of projects, include time for yourself. Women tend to schedule their own needs last. There are always so many demands, and you never really get through them all — so you might as well put yourself on that list somewhere. You may need to meet a friend for coffee, or have your nails done, or simply move away from the phone and take a catnap. (My mother has always had the ability to stop midway through the day and actually sleep for 15 minutes, then continue on the remainder of the day refreshed, and in top form.)

Allow me also to encourage you to get into a routine of attending church regulary. Church affords an opportune time to regroup and put your life into perspective on a weekly basis. In addition, you will make lasting friendships with other young couples that you will treasure for years. But, most importantly, through regular worship, you will gain spiritual enrichment and encouragement that are so vital to the stability of your marriage and your own life.

Here is a list of additional methods for organization that have helped me to run a smoother household with less risk of stress. I admit, however, that I learned some of these the hard way; perhaps I can save you the trouble.

- Acquire a large calendar with ample room to write in dates and obligations. To me, this is a *must*! Then, keep it in a obvious place that is in full view. (I keep mine on the front of the refrigerator.) At the beginning of each week, look over the calendar with your husband. This will help you both avoid slip-ups, and you will be able to stay in communication with one another concerning upcoming events and scheduling. Make it a practice to consult your spouse before accepting social engagements; he will surely appreciate this simple courtesy. You might also follow up with a brief phone call the day of a special event, and merely say how much you are looking forward to accompanying him that evening. He will enjoy hearing it, and it will also be a subtle way to insure that he remembers the date.

- Keep a list of frequently called businesses, such as for your appliance repair services, dog groomer, carpet cleaner, beauty shop, electrician, plumber, yard crew, or any others you use on a regular basis. Keep them near your phone for easy access. (I tend to put things off when I have to make too large an effort finding numbers and information.)

- Keep a list of special dates you wish to acknowledge annually, such as birthdays and anniversaries. Nothing makes you feel as heartsick as does forgetting a special occasion you intended to acknowledge.

- Place a key holder near the door or kitchen for all necessary keys. You will save yourself from the trouble of "lost keys" every time you turn around.

- Provide a "bill box" in a convenient place — perhaps on a desk or in the kitchen. Each day, sort through the mail. Discard junk mail and place bills in the proper box. This only requires seconds to do, but will save you the hassle of having lost important items when you need them.

- A stress-saver box is a necessity for a woman who desires to remain calm amid the stresses in life. My box contains scotch tape, scissors, postage stamps, gift wrapping paper, bows, note cards, stationery, envelopes, and all-occasion cards. (I like to have all-occasion cards on hand in case I don't have a chance to select a particular card. It is better than no card or note at all.) In addition, I always keep my eyes open for "just the right card" for someone special. I have been known to purchase a card for a loved one months in advance, simply because I saw it, and knew it would be appropriate when the time came to give it.

- Sewing boxes, of course, are quite handy for extra buttons, thread, needles, straight pins, safety pins and hooks. Be certain to keep a variety of thread colors and button sizes for "spur of the moment" needs.

- Compile a small, simple first-aid kit. You will want to include items such as bandaids, thermometer, cotton, adhesive tape, sterile gauze pads, antiseptic ointment, tweezers, scissors, and eye lotion.

- Gather a few gift items to have on hand. (Sometimes, I will see a darling baby gift that has been marked down significantly, so I will purchase it for a future shower.) You can do the same for wedding gifts, too. When you have the time, and want to shop for someone specifically, you may do so. But when your circumstances do not allow you to shop, you will still have adequate gift items on hand.

My grandmother was a wonderful bread baker. She made her own breads every week, and would serve her delicious loaves on a lovely pewter bread plate. She made a tradition, during all of her years, of giving a pewter bread plate to nearly every new bride. It was a lovely custom, but also simplified the problem of what to give for most bridal showers.

A few more words to the wise about organization are in order. Be sure to "turn off" your homemaking job for a quiet time, perhaps in the evening, with your mate. Do not allow your days and nights to run together. You both need the regularly scheduled time to exchange thoughts and ideas, and to remain close and content. Always include some of those great "snuggle" times. They are priceless, and are one of the best parts of being married.

Periodically, reevaluate your goals, where you've been, and the direction you want to go. It is a shame to lose sight of worthy, well-thought-out plans. Set several small goals instead of one that is too large and overwhelming; it will only lead you to discouragement.

As a girl of eight, I learned this lesson. Frequently, I visited a neighbor lady, Jane Loffer, who lived on a farm down the road from ours. During the long, hot summers when I had little to do, I would visit with Jane as she worked about in the kitchen. One day while I visited her, she was cleaning strawberries that she had raised in her garden. She must have had a large amount of them, but she kept them in the pantry closet, and took out one large bowl of them at a time. We sat at the table and chatted while she completed each bowl; then she would get up again to refill it from the pantry. I was very curious about her many trips back and forth, so I asked her why she didn't keep the whole container of strawberries by the table. She responded in a way that has stayed in my mind all this time. "Why, child," she said, "if I saw all those strawberries at once, I would never have the courage to even begin such a task." As long as she was only confronted with one bowl at a time, she was able to cope with them. Life can be a lot like Jane's strawberries!

~ *Money Management* ~

Financial problems and disagreements can be the root of many problems in marriage. There are probably more fights between a husband and wife concerning money than any other topic. Marriage counselors even stress that the subject of money often is as important as sex to a sound marriage. Financial goal setting and financial planning should be family ventures. If you and your husband do not agree on decisions about money, your monetary strategy is doomed. But it is hard to stray from a budget that both parties establish together.

Budgeting, of course, is essential. A budget is a statement of estimated income, with a plan for dividing that income for spending and saving. Determine how you are going to use you money; exercise common sense. Plan your expenditures carefully, setting both short-term and long-term goals.

Family household responsiblities are many and varied. You may classify them in the following categories:

- Food

- Housing — including utilities, etc.

- Automobile or Transportation

- Clothing

- Recreation

- Savings

- Miscellaneous — spending money, gifts, etc.

The great percentage of personal expense, such as food, rent, and utilities, occurs on a regular basis. Plan ahead, however, for the irregular ones, such as auto insurance and taxes. Set aside a little each month to meet large bills that may occur annually or semi-annually.

Unforeseen expenses can also be a problem for your budget. Consider the possibilty of having to meet a large medical expense or major car repair. For this reason, you need an emergency fund. Financial advisors recommend keeping enough in your savings to live on for three to six months. Once you have acquired this emergency fund, you can begin to save toward larger investments and long-term savings. Get in the habit now of saving money. Learn to pay yourself first; when you get your paycheck, take out the predetermined amount you are to save and put it away immediately before anything can happen to it. Small sums invested regularly can grow into a substantial nest egg. Even a passbook savings account, with $50.00 invested every two weeks at a 5.5% annual interest rate, (compounded daily), will add up to $1337 at the end of one year, $2751 at the end of two years, and $7490 at the end of five years.

Tiny savings can add up, too. For example, if you use food coupons and brown bag your lunch, you might pocket an additional $30 or more per week.

Credit allows you to enjoy many items much sooner than if you had to save the money before making the purchase — but credit carries with it certain costs and obligations. Be careful not to over-extend yourself; every day people abuse credit. Being hounded by bill collectors and being unable to meet commitments is a frightening experience.

Credit cards (a convenient form of credit) are wonderful to have, but also dangerous. First, do not acquire too many of them. Keep only one or two major ones. Do not carry them with you unless you have great self-control; they can be quite a tempation. Besides, if you do not pay off your balance each month, you are paying much too much in interest. The majority of bank credit cards charge from 18.6% to 22% per year. The best way to save money is to pay the total balance owed, and to pay it on time. That way, you will not pay any interest at all. If you have, for example, a running balance of $1,000 per month, and pay an interest rate of 21%, that card will cost you $210 a year (not counting the annual membership fee). Some banks now offer credit cards at a reduced rate of interest. Shop around for the lowest rate you can find; then remember to pay your balance each month in full, whenever possible.

Keep your monthly bills in a specific place as you receive them. Also, keep a supply of postage stamps and envelopes. Give attention to the due dates of your bills and pay them on time! This will enable you to build a good credit rating as well as to save money by avoiding late charges. I like to keep my bills filed in the order of their due dates. Then, I sit down only once a month to write out the bills, and place them in envelopes ready to mail. On the back corner of each envelope, in tiny numbers, I put the date each letter should be mailed in order to reach its destination on time (and avoid penalties). I then place the bills in the order of their mailing dates. This way, I am able to complete all the month's bills, although I may not as yet have the funds to pay them. Each payday, I look to see which bills need to be put in the mailbox for that time period.

Do yourself a huge favor, and keep accurate records of all check writing. Each time you write a check, *immediately* record the amount, date and check number. Keep your balance up to date, never guessing how much your reserve might be. It is a sickening experience to receive a returned check marked "insufficient funds" and also have to pay the overdraft fee of $15 to $20 charged by your bank.

Consider, also, that money management for the family is not determined by gender, but by the partner most able to handle the responsibility of money. Decide which one of you will keep the records and make out the bills, although both partners should always be informed and aware of the financial status at any given time. It is not recommended that both you and your husband carry checkbooks of the same account. Such an arrangement seldom works, because checks that are written are not always recorded properly (usually one partner forgets to tell the other).

Yes, money matters are time-consuming and require a great deal of thought and much communication. When dealing with two salaries, money management is even more difficult. You must take the time to talk it out together; only then can you be successful. Agree upon your goals as a couple. Each month, put your monies together toward these goals and toward what you expect to achieve as a team effort. Also set aside a certain amount of spending money for each of you. As individuals, you deserve some money for yourselves, individually. Keep a certain amount of cash tucked away in your billfold for an emergency, such as taxi fare home when the car breaks down. It is also good to have money of your own when you want to buy something special for your spouse; or to treat yourself to something like a new hair-do.

If you are a working wife, let me caution you against depending too heavily on your own income. I prefer to think of the wife's income being used for extra purchases, luxuries, vacations, additional savings, or home furnishings. Try not to count on your salary for mortgage payments, groceries, and ongoing expenses. You may want to start a family, later, and find yourselves in a position financially that would not allow you to live on one salary. That is why good, sound financial planning is so very important. You need to be able to look down the road a ways. Admittedly, it takes a great deal of time to develop the right systematic approach to caring for your financial circumstances, but you will never regret the time and effort when you see the progress you make. To sum it up: Plan your expenditures carefully, spend your money wisely, and invest your savings sensibly.

. . . But
Can She
Cook?

Cooking Skills

Getting Started

Equipping the Kitchen

Grocery Shopping

Kitchen Knowledge

Recipes That Really Work

The barber and the piano player had to eat. . . . I could also call this section "and the two shall become one."

It's difficult to think of cooking when you have just smiled through hundreds of dollars of silk and satin and watched your mother and your mother-in-law smile at each other while your new husband is being patted on the back by every male over sixteen.

Limos, three-tiered cakes, and candles that glow — surely this moment will last forever, as your best friend from school sings "Forever and Always."

Indeed, it does. Approximately 271,560 hours later, I still remember the day the barber said "I do." Now let me wipe my eyes and get back to the point! I was cute, he was handsome, and we made beautiful music together. Even so, we both got hungry, and the wedding cake was gone.

Although this book is my gift to young brides, I strongly advise you and your new husband to read and enact this section together, from setting up the kitchen to making sure that you both know a few standard recipes that really work.

But can she cook? Of course — both can. And isn't it romantic? After all, you both need to know what a nest of cups is all about.

Cooking Skills

~ Getting Started ~

This section is, without a doubt, the most exciting part of the book for me because I do *love* cooking — not simply for the necessity of it, but for the pure joy I derive from it. When I am tired, full of stress, or upset, I can get busy in my kitchen, stir some things up, and leave my woes behind. What therapy it can be! It gives me a peace and relaxation in which I can lose myself.

On the other hand, when I feel energetic and want to be constructive, I am again drawn to the kitchen. I might read through new recipes, create one, or bake something for a friend in need. Thus, it seems that cooking is a vital part of my life, whether my emotions are up *or* down.

I've heard it so many times: The kitchen is the heart of the home. I truly believe that myself; it applies to mine. I hope that you, too, can become more and more comfortable in your kitchen, and gain from it some of the same satisfactions that I have. I trust that it will be a pleasure for you to create nutritious and tasty dishes that you can share with those who mean so very much to you. What better way to demonstrate your love for them?

There is no better time than now to get started. You will be delighted when you create delicious meals in your very own home. I assure you that cooking is one of the most appreciated and useful skills you can acquire. Given a little time and determination, you can learn to cook well. If at first you do not succeed, keep trying; you will see improvement daily. Be sure to rejoice when the successes come, but don't be too discouraged when the results fall short of your expectations. (I can recall vividly some of my first attempts at cooking. I knew next to nothing; more than once my failures were poured down the drain. But a desire to do better always kept me going.)

In retropect, one of the funniest incidents from my early years as a homemaker occurred when Ed went dove hunting. It was his first hunting trip after our wedding, and it was a custom that I was not familiar with. When he returned home later that day, I was away. He placed the still-feathered birds on the kitchen countertop and proceeded to take a shower before cleaning them. In the meantime, I returned home. Upon seeing the little creatures in my kitchen, I assumed that Ed left them there so that I could admire his trophies — the successes of his hunting skills. After taking a few quick glancs at them, I neatly wrapped them in newspaper and placed them outside in the garbage can. By this time, Ed had showered and was ready to clean his birds and prepare them for cooking. Much to his dismay, they were gone. "Where are my doves?" he enquired furiously. I proudly answered him with the explanation that I had already seen them and discarded them. "What do you mean, discard?" he yelled. "We eat the game I bring in this house!" You can be assured that I learned a very quick lesson in cooking — that of frying dove for a meal! (It was good; but quail are the best, I was later to learn!)

As you are learning to cook, always follow directions *to the letter.* Later, you can begin to experiment and give your creativity free rein. Also, before you begin to prepare a dish, check to be sure that you have all of the necessary ingredients. There is nothing as disgusting as getting halfway through a recipe and finding that you lack one ingredient.

The method in which you measure ingredients can make the difference between success and failure of your cooking. For instance, to measure brown sugar accurately, pack it lightly so that it holds the shape of the cup when you turn it out. To measure liquids, use a standard glass or clear plastic measuring cup with a spout. Place it on a level surface; bend down so the marking for the amount you need is at eye level. To measure dry ingredients, use a dry measuring cup that holds the exact amount you need. Lightly spoon in the ingredient; then level it with a flat-bladed metal spatula or the straight edge of a dinner knife. Do not dip a measuring cup into the flour; you'll pack in more flour than you need.

When I begin to prepare a meal, I quickly set the table first. This immediately sets the mood for a meal in the making. Not only does it inspire you, the cook, but it also reassures a hungry husband, just walking through the door, that dinner is not long from being ready. What encouragement to a hungry stomach! (A little trick I learned very early in marriage.)

No matter how simple the meal you are preparing, you, your husband, and guests will enjoy it even more if the table looks inviting and the food is served attractively. This does not not mean you have to have the finest in tablewear. Creativity on your part will go a long way. Make a practice of doing things nicely on a daily basis — not only will your family enjoy it, but giving a dinner party will present few added difficulties because you will have been doing things nicely all along.

COMMON COOKING TERMS

Baste	Spoon a liquid over food during baking to keep it moist.
Beat	To mix vigorously until mixture is smooth.
Blanch	Plunge food into boiling water for a brief time.
Boil	Heat until bubbles rise continuously and break on the surface of liquid.
Chop (Dice)	Cut into irregular pieces about the size of peas.
Cube	Cut into small squares.
Fold	To mix gently with down, across, up and over motion.
Saute	To brown in a small amount of cooking oil or margarine.
Scald	To bring liquid to temperature just below the boiling point. (Tiny bubbles appear around the sides of the surface.)

Simmer	Cook in liquid just below the boiling point.
Steam	To cook by contact with live steam in a closed container.
Stew	To simmer slowly in a small amount of liquid.
Stir	To mix ingredients with a circular motion until well blended.
Whip	To beat rapidly so as to incorporate air and increase volume. (usually in heavy cream and egg whites)

MEASURING INGREDIENTS

Measuring tools are a must in any kitchen for consistent cooking results. Individual measuring cups are for dry ingredients; glass measuring cups with pouring spouts are for liquid ingredients. Measuring spoons are for both liquid and dry ingredients.

 For flour, granulated sugar, baking mixes, and powdered sugar, spoon lightly into cup and level with straight-edged knife.

 For soft bread crumbs, shredded cheese, chopped nuts, and coconut, spoon into cup and pack lightly.

 For shortening and brown sugar, spoon into cup and pack down firmly. Then level with straight-edged knife.

 To measure liquids in glass cup, place cup on flat surface and read markings at eye level.

~ *Equipping the Kitchen* ~

The simple, basic items will suffice for your kitchen, although sophisticated department stores would not have you believe so. You do not need a lot of fancy appliances to get started cooking. I have included a list of what I consider the essentials needed to prepare most meals. Much of it can simply be purchased at a variety store or even at your grocery store.

KITCHEN UTENSILS

paring knife
carving knife
slicing knife
serrated knife
potato masher
pancake turner
pastry blender
glass measuring cup
   (for liquid)
nest of dry
measuring cups
nest of measuring
   spoons
set of mixing bowls
stainless steel mixing
   bowls
cast-iron skillets (a
   must)

heavy aluminum
   saucepan
teflon skillet (for
   eggs)
teflon egg turner
rolling pin
portable mixer
can opener
biscuit cutter
lemon squeezer
strainer
colander
spatulas
vegetable brush
wooden spoons
coffee maker
cooling rack
set of saucepans

kitchen scissors
steamer basket
dutch oven
baking pans
loaf pan
tongs
whisk
grater
timer
baking sheet
pie pans
muffin tin
hot pads
dish towels
pot holders
cookbooks

~ Grocery Shopping ~

It is wise to plan your menus carefully, with a well thought-out grocery list, before you go to the food market. You may be slow at this task at first, but before long you will get into a routine of it. It is best to shop regularly, such as once a week. Know how many meals you will be planning, and how much of your budget is to cover grocery items. Specify whether that amount is to include drug items, toiletries, cleaning supplies, or others. Decide on the amount budgeted and stay within your boundaries. Purchase necessities only. Never shop when you are hungry, and don't shop with friends. Either way, you can easily overspend. For additional savings, use coupons, but only for products you normally buy.

ADDITIONAL SUGGESTIONS

- Keep a memo pad handy in both your kitchen and bathroom

- Group items on your list as they are organized in the store, to avoid back-tracking

- Read labels, know what you are getting

- Shop early in the day or the middle of the week to avoid crowds

- Use in-season foods to save money

- If you have a freezer, take advantage of sale items

- Clean and reorganize your refrigerator each time you shop

- Stock newly purchased food items behind previously purchased ones

- Keep plenty of potatoes on hand; they have many uses

- Put perishable food items in your cart last, to insure that they retain cold temperature enroute to your home

As you plan your shopping, strive to include plenty of the most nutritious foods. The ones listed below are certainly quite nutritional and are thought to be cancer preventive as well:

Broccoli	Peaches
Cauliflower	Apricots
Carrots	Strawberries
Brussel Sprouts	Oranges
Squash	Cantaloupe
Green Peppers	High Fiber Foods
Cabbage	Rice

I have also included a list of basic staples for setting up housekeeping:

Vegetable Shortening	Cornstarch
Cooking Oil	Coffee, Tea
Flour — unbleached, whole-wheat	Cocoa
	Milk — powdered, canned
Sugar — granulated, powdered, brown	Soups
	Corn Meal
	Pickles, Relishes
Spices	Mayonnaise, Mustard
Flavoring Extracts	Worcestershire Sauce
Salt, Pepper	Kitchen Bouquet
Honey	Cereals, Rice
Syrup, Jellies	Baking Powder
Peanut Butter	Baking Soda
Pastas — noodles, spaghetti, macaroni	

I offer several recipes in this book; they include only ones that I have used over and over again. Many have been contributed by family and friends over the years. Other have been exchanged at some delightful church dinners. I believe that they are dependable and will offer you a good base from which to start. In the meantime, let me encourage you to compile a recipe box of your own. Every time you eat something you really enjoy, get the recipe and add it to your file. It won't take long for you to accumulate a wonderful variety of tested recipes that fit your taste. When you try unknown ones from cookbooks, rate the recipe from one to ten in the margin of the book. Then you will always remember which recipes you have tried and how well you like them.

When you are preparing meals, get in the habit of putting away ingredients as you use them. It will make clean-up time much easier, and you will not find yourself suddenly in a messy kitchen.

The next section reviews basic cooking knowledge. Most cookbooks assume that you know these basics. (Speaking of cookbooks, invest in several very good "general" ones.) The cookbook I have depended on the most is *Better Homes and Gardens New Cookbook*. Other personal favorites are *The Betty Crocker Cookbook*, and *The Southern Living Cookbook*.

~ *Kitchen Knowledge* ~

- Egg whites can be kept frozen as long as a year. Collect them for angel food cakes.

- To keep egg yolks from crumbling when slicing hard boiled ones, wet the knife before each cut.

- Use copper or stainless steel bowls for whipping egg whites.

- For recipes using beaten egg whites, the eggs should be separated while cold, but the whites should reach room temperature before beating; this insures fullest volume.

- When beating egg whites, the bowl and beaters must be free of any trace of oil or the egg whites will not fluff up.

- When whipping cream, place waxed paper over the bowl; tear a hole in the middle of the paper for the beaters. This will keep cream from splattering.

- Cream whipped ahead of time will not separate if you add ¼ teaspoon of unflavored gelatin per cup of cream.

- Cream will whip faster if bowl and beaters are chilled first.

- Mound left-over whipping cream on waxed paper placed on cookie sheet; freeze until firm, then place in plastic bags for use on your next dessert. (allow 15 minutes to thaw)

- Remove corn silk with a damp paper towel and brush downward on the corn cob.

- Eliminate fat from soup or broth by dropping in ice cupes; the fat will cling to the cubes.

- Store lemons in a tightly sealed jar of water; they will yield more juice.

- Cooking in cast-iron utensils greatly increases your iron intake.

- A fresh pineapple is ripe when the leaves at the top pull out easily.

- Store cooked spaghetti in a stainless steel bowl covered with water in refrigerator. When ready to use, place in a sieve or colander, dip in boiling water (with a little cooking oil and salt) a few minutes.

- Wash dry beans before cooking; they are usually full of dirt. (Place beans in a sieve and run water over them.)

- Place baked potatoes in a muffin tin; this keeps them from rolling over in the oven and also makes them easier to remove from the oven.

- Always date everything you put in your freezer.

- When tomatoes or avocadoes are not quite ripe, place them in a paper bag under cabinet in a dark place; check in 2-3 days.

- Clean celery by snapping off large end; most of the strands will peel off.

- Food is not as likely to stick to the skillet if skillet is hot before you add the food.

- Keep lettuce longer by storing in paper bags instead of plastic ones.

- To prevent sticky noodles, macaroni and spaghetti, add a little cooking oil to the water.

- When you have extra tomatoes from the garden, you may freeze them sliced or whole on a cookie sheet; then place in plastic bag.

- Save your cookbook by keeping a piece of plastic wrap in it. Cover the page you're working from with the plastic to avoid spills on the pages.

- Purchase unfolded cloth baby diapers for great kitchen drying towels.

- Grade your recipes from 1 to 10 in the margin; then you will always know which recipes you liked best.

- For easy peeling of tomatoes, peaches and plums, place them briefly in boiling water, then cold water.

- When mashing potatoes, don't throw away the cooking water — it contains many of the nutrients. Mix it with dry milk and use in potatoes.

- Most refrigerated foods keep longer in glass jars than in plastic containers.

- Roast meats at a slightly lower temperature (300° instead of 350°) for juicer and more tender results; the meat also will shrink less.

- Spices lose their flavor in time; date them when you purchase them and discard after about a year.

- To reheat refrigerated rice, put in a vegetable steamer with a tight-fitting lid; you'll have fluffy, hot rice in minutes.

- When you have extra bananas, they can be stored in the freezer; peel them or not, but use later in recipes calling for mashed or chunked bananas.

- To keep cookies moist, place an apple piece in the bottom of the cookie jar.

- To prevent browning when working with a quantity of peeled apples, slice them into water with one tablespoon of fresh lemon juice.

- Store cottage cheese upside down in its carton; it will keep twice as long.

- Bake cakes in a shiny metal pan with a non-stick finish. If you must use glass, reduce temperature of oven by 25°.

- Soften hardened brown sugar by placing a slice of soft bread or half of an apple in the package and closing tightly.

- You will shed fewer tears while chopping onions if you freeze or refrigerate them first.

- Ripen green bananas by wrapping them in a wet dish towel and placing them in a paper sack.

- Spray your molds with Pam™ to help you unmold them later.

- Make colored sugar to decorate cookies by dropping 1-3 drops of food coloring in a jar with ¼ cup granulated sugar; shake.

- Cover the surface of cooked puddings and pie fillings with plastic wrap to prevent skin-like film from forming.

- You can tell whether eggs are fresh by placing them in a deep pan of water; eggs that float to the top should be discarded and the ones on the bottom are fine to use.

- To prevent cheese from drying out in the refrigerator, wrap a moistened paper towel around it, then place in a plastic bag and tie shut.

- Keep cheese longer and avoid mold by moistening a paper towel with cider vinegar; wrap the towel around the cheese and place in a sealed plastic bag.

- Always wipe your rolling pin off with a dry towel; do not immerse in water.

- Purchase a box of inexpensive sandwich bags for hundreds of uses.

- Rinse out chicken and other meat wrappings before discarding into trash, to reduce odor.

- Insert paper plates between fine china plates to prevent scratches.

- Put a thin layer of water in the broiling pan before using to make pan easier to clean later; it also keeps pan from smoking while broiling.

- Cut off box tops of aluminum foil, plastic wrap and waxed paper so they will fit better in your drawer and be more convenient to use.

- Broccoli should be cooked in a covered pan, but remove the lid several times during cooking to help keep broccoli green.

- When washing fine china and crystal, place a towel on the bottom of sink or use a rubber dishpan.

- To help glasses and silverware shine, add a capful of liquid bleach or ammonia to the dishwater; use rubber gloves to save your hands.

- Vinegar is a must when rinsing crystal; use one part vinegar with three parts water.

- A small nick in the rim of a glass can be smoothed out with an emery board.

- Use salt or baking soda to extinguish kitchen fires.

- Remove tops of carrots before storing; they will keep longer.

- For a cake decorator, use a plastic bag and cut off one corner, or use a plastic mustard or ketsup dispenser.

- Pure honey eventually granulates. To restore to liquid state, place container in very hot water, but not boiling; overheating will spoil the flavor.

~ *Recipes That Really Work* ~

MAIN DISHES

TENDER ROAST BEEF

Purchase about a 3 lb. boneless chuck roast. Brown both sides in a heavy skillet (I prefer a cast-iron skillet) in about 1½ tablespoon of oil. Then place roast on a sheet of aluminum foil, season with black pepper, and wrap *tightly*. Put wrapped roast in a shallow baking pan and bake at 300° for about 3 hours. When roast is done, allow the juices in the foil to leak out into the baking pan; remove roast from pan but keep in foil so it will remain warm and not dry out. For a good roast gravy, add about 2 cups of water to the meat juices. (also scrape any brown particles on the bottom of pan into the liquid for additional flavor.) Pour the liquid into a large glass; when slightly cooled, skim off any fat that forms on top.

Reheat the skillet that you browned the roast in; add 2 T. oil and 2 T. flour. Cook and stir until mixture is somewhat brown, smooth, and bubbly. Remove from heat and pour in most of the liquid; return to heat and stir until thickened, gradually adding more liquid if needed. Add salt and pepper to taste. For an even browner, more flavorful gravy, add 2 t. Kitchen Bouquet (a browning and seasoning sauce).

TASTY FRIED CHICKEN

One 2½- to 3-lb. broiler-fryer chicken, cut up, or selected chicken pieces.

buttermilk, about 1 cup

flour, about 1 cup

salt/pepper

shortening for frying

Dip chicken in buttermilk; coat with flour. In a large, heavy skillet, melt shortening to about 1 inch in depth. When shortening is quite hot, place chicken pieces in skillet; do not overcrowd. Sprinkle generously with salt and pepper. Brown chicken on both sides; reduce heat and cover tightly. Simmer for about 30 minutes turning once. Uncover, turn heat up some and cook about 10 more minutes or until chicken is crispy. Drain on paper towels. (to test doneness, pierce chicken with a fork)

CHICKEN CREAM GRAVY

Pour off all but about 4 T. of the drippings. Add 6 T. of flour. Cook over medium heat, stirring until mixture is smooth and bubbly. Remove from heat; pour in about 3 cups of milk. Return to heat and stir until thickened and smooth. Gradually add more milk if gravy is too thick. Season with salt and pepper.

GOULASH

1 lb. ground beef

½ onion, chopped

1 can (28 oz) whole peeled tomatoes

1 t. sugar

salt, pepper

macaroni, 5-6 oz.

½ cup sliced ripe olives

Mozzarella cheese, 4 oz.

Cook the ground beef and onion in a large skillet until the beef is browned and the onion is tender. Pour off any grease. Add the can of tomatoes and chop them up slightly; sprinkle sugar over the tomatoes. Add about ⅓ cup of water also. Cook macaroni as directed on package; drain off water and add the beef mixture.

Season with salt and pepper; add the olives and a pat of butter. Heat thoroughly; place cheese on top, cover tightly until cheese melts.

POT ROAST MEATLOAF

Mix together:
> 1 lb. hamburger
> ⅔ cup milk
> ⅓ cup dry bread crumbs or oats
> ¼ cup ketchup
> 2 t. Worcestershire sauce
> ¼ t. pepper

Shape into loaf in center of baking pan. Around the loaf place
> potatoes, peeled and quartered
> carrots, cut in chunks
> onions, quartered

Cover pan and bake in oven at 350° for 30 minutes. Uncover and bake an additional 5 minutes. (leftovers make delicious sandwiches)

CHICKEN TETRAZZINI PRESTO

> 7 oz. package *cut* spaghetti
> 2 cans Swanson's™ chicken a la king
> 1 small jar sliced mushrooms, drained
> 2 T. butter or margarine
> ⅓ cup milk
> ½ t. onion salt
> ¼ t. pepper
> 4 oz. sharp cheddar cheese, grated

Cook spaghetti and drain well. Combine with remaining ingredients except cheese. Pour into a buttered 2-quart baking dish and bake at 350° for about 25 minutes or until hot and bubbly. Add cheese on top and bake 5 more minutes.

NOTE: This mixture can be halved — pour into two small baking dishes; bake one and freeze one for later.

BUSY-DAY ROAST

3 lb. roast

⅓ bottle A-1™ sauce

1 small can of mushrooms, drained

1 envelope dry onion soup mix

1 can cream of mushroom soup

Place roast in baking pan; mix remaining ingredients and pour over roast. Cover tightly and bake at 325° for 3 hours.

DRIP BEEF SANDWICHES

3-4 lb. arm or chuck roast

⅓ t. oregano

¾ t. seasoned salt

1 T. garlic salt

¼ t. rosemary

2 beef bouillon cubes

Trim fat from roast. Put in dutch oven and add water to just cover roast. Add seasonings; cover and cook on top of stove for eight hours on lowest heat. Shred beef with 2 forks and serve on buns. Use broth for dipping.

CAROLYN'S WILD RICE HOT DISH

1 lb. hamburger meat

2 cups wild rice

½ lb. chopped bacon

1 cup celery, chopped

1 cup onion, chopped

1 small green pepper, chopped

1 t. salt

½ t. pepper

1 can cream of mushroom soup

dash of marjoram

Wash 2 cups wild rice well. Soak for a couple hours in 2 quarts warm water. Fry the bacon until crisp and set aside. In bacon drippings, saute celery, onion, green pepper until about half done; add hamburger to vegetable mixture and cook only until browned. Add salt and pepper.

Add the drained rice to 3 quarts boiling water and let come to a boil. Shut off heat and let stand for 10 minutes. Drain, then add the vegetable-meat mixture; fold in soup and marjoram. Bake in a covered dish at 350° for 1 hour. Serve as a main dish or a side dish.

LAZY LADY'S CHICKEN

4 chicken pieces

1 T. oil

2 onions, quartered

3 carrots, scraped and chunked

2 potatoes, chunked

1 cup chicken broth

2 T. white wine

1 T. chopped parsley

Brown chicken in oil; remove to greased 8x8 dish-skin up. Between chicken pieces, stuff vegetables. Pour broth and wine over all. Sprinkle with parsley and bake at 400° for 45 minutes.

CREOLE FLOUNDER

1 lb. flounder fillets, cut into serving-size
  portions

1 tomato, chopped

½ green pepper, chopped

3 T. lemon juice

1½ t. vegetable oil

1 t. salt

1 t. onion, finely chopped

½ t. dried basil leaves

⅛ t. pepper

1 drop red pepper sauce

Place fish in greased oblong baking dish. Mix remaining ingredients and spoon onto fish. Cook uncovered in oven at 400° until fish flakes easily with fork, about 10 minutes. Garnish with green pepper rings and tomato wedges. (4 servings)

FISH IN FOIL

The delicious flavor of tender fish contained in foil

¾ lb. fish fillets

½ t. salt

⅛ t. pepper

2 T. margarine, melted

1 T. parsley, chopped

½ T. lemon juice

½ t. salt

¼ t. dill weed

1 T. oil

2 slices onion, thinly sliced

½ cup carrots, thinly sliced

2 slices Swiss cheese

Cut fish into 2 servings pieces and sprinkle with ½ t. salt and ⅛ t. pepper. Combine margarine, parsley, lemon juice, salt and dill weed. Cut 2 pieces of foil in about 10x12 inches each and brush with oil. Place 1 t. of the margarine mixture on each piece of foil; place fish on top and cover with onion and carrots. Pour remaining margarine mixture on top of fish and add slice of cheese. Fold the foil together and seal on top. Place the foil cases on a baking pan and bake at 400° for 35 minutes, or until fish flakes easily with a fork.

HAMBURGER CASSEROLE

8 oz. noodles

1 lb. lean hamburger

2 cans (8 oz each) tomato sauce

8 oz. cottage cheese

1 package (8 oz) cream cheese

¼ cup sour cream

⅓ green onion, chopped

2 T. margarine, melted

¼ cup Parmesan cheese

Cook noodles according to package and drain. Saute hamburger until brown and drain off any fat. Stir in tomato sauce and remove from heat. Combine cheeses, sour cream, and green onion. Spread ½ of the noodles in a 2-quart casserole dish and cover with the cheese mixture; cover with remaining noodles. Pour melted margarine over the noodles; pour meat sauce over all. Top with Parmesan cheese and bake at 375° for 40 minutes. (Makes about 8 servings, so you may want to divide recipe and freeze half of it for later. Then use 2 one-quart baking dishes)

HEARTY BEEF STEW

1 lb. stew meat (boneless roast cut into
1-inch cubes)

1 T. shortening

½ onion, sliced

¼ t. pepper

5 cups hot water

* * * *

3 carrots, cut into ½-inch pieces

1 potato, cut into 1-inch pieces

2 stalks celery, cut into ½-inch pieces

½ onion chopped

½ t. salt

½ t. pepper

1 t. Kitchen Bouquet seasoning

Melt shortening in a Dutch oven; add stew meat and cook until well browned. Add the sliced onion, pepper, and water. Heat to boiling; reduce heat. Cover tightly and simmer for about 2 hours, or until meat is almost tender.

Add the vegetables, salt, and pepper. Cover and simmer an additional 30-40 minutes or until vegetables and meat are quite tender.

Pour off and reserve the liquid from the stew. In a skillet melt 2 T. shortening and stir in 4-5 T. flour. Stir over medium heat until mixture is smooth and light brown. Remove from heat, pour in reserved liquid, stirring well. Return to heat and cook until mixture is smooth and slightly thickened; add more water if needed, since consistency should not be quite as thick as gravy (meat and vegetables will already make it thicker). Stir in salt, pepper, and Kitchen Bouquet. Pour over meat and vegetables in Dutch oven and stir to blend. Serve with cornbread muffins.

CREAMED BEEF OVER TOAST
(A Jiffy Dish!)

In a skillet, mix together 3 T. oil with 5 T. flour; heat and stir until smooth and bubbly. Remove from heat and add 3 cups milk. Return to heat, bring to a boil and stir constantly until sauce is smooth and thickened. Turn down heat; add a small jar of dried beef, tearing into smaller pieces. Add pepper but no salt as the dried beef is already quite salty. Remove from heat and serve over hot buttered toast.

CREAMED CHICKEN OVER BISCUITS

Cook a small fryer in a Dutch oven, covering the chicken with water. Cook covered on low heat for about 1½ hours. Bone and cube the chicken, but reserve about 3 cups of the broth. After the broth is cool, skim off the fat on top. In a skillet, mix together 3 T. oil with 5 T. flour and cook over medium heat unitl hot and bubbly. Remove from heat; add 2 chicken bouillon cubes and the 3 cups of chicken broth. Bring to a boil, stirring constantly, until mixture is thickened and cubes are dissolved. Turn down heat; add chicken. Salt and pepper to taste and serve over hot homemade biscuits.

Biscuits: Mix together 1 cup flour, 2 teaspoons baking powder, ¼ teaspoon salt, ¼ teaspoon cream of tarter, and 1 teaspoon of sugar. With a pastry blender, cut in ¼ cup shortening until all of the flour mixture is *completely* blended with shortening. Make a well in the center; pour in ⅓ cup milk all at once. Stir quickly with a fork until dough follows fork around bowl. Turn dough onto a lightly floured surface and knead about 10 strokes.

Pat dough ½ inch thick; dip biscuit cutter into flour and cut out biscuits. Bake on ungreased pan at 450° for about 10 minutes. Makes about 8 small biscuits.

SALADS AND SOUPS

APPLESAUCE SALAD

1 package (3oz) lime jello

1 can applesauce

2 T. lemon juice

1 can (12 oz) 7-up

Heat applesauce and dissolve jello in it. Add lemon juice and 7-up. Pour into mold and chill.

FIVE CUP SALAD

1 cup sour cream

1 cup mandarin oranges

1 cup crushed pineapple

1 cup coconut

1 cup miniature marshmallows

Mix all ingredients and chill throughly.

TOSSED SALAD

½ head lettuce, torn in pieces

1 stalk celery, chopped

1 carrot, grated

1 green onion, sliced

½ cup fresh mushrooms, sliced

¼ cup Cheddar cheese, grated

Toss all ingredients together and serve with dressing below:

Dressing: Mix together ½ cup mayonnaise, ½ cup sour cream, 4 T. milk, ½ t. pepper, ½ t. salt, and ¼ t. garlic powder. Blend thoroughly; chill; use amount needed for salad and store the rest for another time.

PINEAPPLE CREAM SALAD

  1 can (20 oz) crushed pineapple

  1 package (3 oz) lemon jello

  1 packaged (8 oz) cream cheese, room temperature

  ½ jar pimento, drained

  1 cup heavy cream, whipped

  1 cup celery, diced

  1 cup pecans, chopped

  pinch salt

Bring pineapple with juice to boil over low heat. Remove from heat and dissolve jello in it; cool. Blend together cream cheese and pimento until smooth. Fold in whipped cream; add celery, nuts, and salt. Mix with first mixture after it is completely cooled. Pour into mold and refrigerate for several hours.

JEANNE'S COLE SLAW

Wash cabbage in ice cold water, shred. Mix with chilled mayonnaise; as you are mixing, sprinkle with sugar. Chill at least three hours before serving.

SEVEN LAYER SALAD

lettuce, torn into bite-size pieces

green pepper, chopped

cucumber, chopped

frozen green peas

mayonnaise

1 T. sugar

Cheddar cheese, grated

bacon bits

Amount of ingredients will be determined by the size of your bowl. Layer in this order: lettuce, green pepper, cucumber and peas. Continue to layer until your bowl is full. Spread a layer of mayonnaise on top; sprinkle with sugar. Top with a layer of Cheddar cheese and crumbled bacon bits. Store in refrigerator until ready to serve; can be prepared a day in advance.

SPICED PEACH SALAD

¼ cup vinegar

¾ cup peach juice

¼ cup sugar

10 cloves

small cinnamon stick

1 package (3 oz) orange jello

1 cup sliced peaches

In a saucepan combine vinegar, peach juice, sugar and spices. Bring to a boil and add peach slices. Simmer 10 minutes and remove spices and peaches. Add enough water to syrup to make 2 cups liquid. Dissolve jello in the boiling liquid. Cool and refrigerate until jello is slightly thickened. Fold in peaches and chill until firmly set. (good with ham)

BROCCOLI SOUP

1½ lbs. fresh broccoli

1 cup onion, finely chopped

1 cup green pepper, chopped

½ cup butter or margarine

⅓ cup flour

4 cups milk

salt/pepper

Wash broccoli; break into flowerets; steam until very tender. Saute onion and green pepper in the butter or margarine. Stir in flour; gradually add milk. Cook and stir until thickened. Add steamed broccoli; season with salt and pepper. (I like to mash part of the broccoli so it blends with the liquid)

TOMATO SOUP

1 cup instant dry milk

1 can (46 oz) tomato juice

2 T. minced dry onion

2 T. fresh parsley, chopped

1 t. white vinegar

½ t. dried basil

½ t. salt

1 bay leaf

2 whole cloves

1 t. sugar

Place milk powder in bowl. Gradually add 1½ cups of the tomato juice; mix well and set aside. In large saucepan, combine remaining juice and other ingredients, except sugar. Simmer for 5-10 minutes; remove bay leaf and cloves. Pour some of the hot liquid into the tomato-milk mixture; pour slowly back to pan. Add sugar last; heat slowly — do not allow to boil.

CAULIFLOWER SOUP

1 medium head of cauliflower

4 cups water

1 onion, chopped

4 chicken bouillon cubes

¼ cup butter or margarine

¼ cup flour

2 cups milk

¼ t. salt

¼ t. nutmeg

¼ t. pepper

¼ Cheddar cheese, shredded

Wash cauliflower and break into flowerettes. Combine water, onion, and bouillon cubes in a large saucepan; bring to boil. Add cauliflower; cover and cook until cauliflower is tender.

Spoon half of cauliflower mixture into blender; blend until smooth. Repeat with the other half of mixture.

Melt butter or margarine in heavy saucepan. Add flour; stir until smooth. Cook one minute; gradually add milk and cook until thickened. Add salt, nutmeg, and pepper.

Return cauliflower mixture to large pan; add white sauce to it. Cook over low heat until well-heated. Serve with cheese sprinkled on top. Makes 5-6 cups.

VEGETABLES

For most vegetable dishes, I prefer using a steamer. Valuable nutrients and color are retained, not to mention the wonderful natural flavor. Nothing tastes better than fresh garden green beans, new potatoes, broccoli, carrots, or squash simply cooked in a steamer. All you need is a steamer basket, the kind you can purchase at most supermarkets. They fold up in a small circle for storage and open to fit various sizes of saucepans. To use, place basket in desired pan with about 1-2 inches of water in the bottom of pan. Place washed vegetable in basket; cover tightly and cook over very low heat until slightly tender. Then add a touch of margarine, salt, and pepper. Or if you like, add a hollandaise sauce.

HOLLANDAISE SAUCE

Stir 3 egg yolks with 1 T. lemon juice vigorously in small saucepan. Add ¼ cup butter and heat over *very low heat*, stirring constantly, until butter is melted. Add another ¼ cup of butter; continue stirring vigorously until butter is melted and sauce is thickened. Serve hot over vegetables. Makes ¾ cup sauce.

MUSTARD GREEN BEANS

1 lb. green beans, cleaned and trimmed

4 t. butter or margarine

4 t. dry mustard

salt; pepper

Steam beans until crisp-tender. Melt butter or margarine in heavy skillet over medium heat. Stir in mustard. Toss beans in mixture to coat and season with salt and pepper.

EASY BAKED BEANS

3 strips bacon

½ green pepper, chopped

⅓ cup onion, chopped

⅓ cup brown sugar

1 can (46 oz) pork and beans

1 t. mustard

⅓ t. garlic powder

⅓ cup ketchup

Saute bacon, green pepper, and onion in little amount of oil; crumble bacon. Combine with remaining ingredients and place in a baking dish. Bake at 350° until hot and bubbly.

BAKED SQUASH

3 cups zucchini, unpared, sliced and steamed until almost tender

1 egg yolk, slighty beaten

½ cup sour cream

1 T. flour

1 egg white, stiffly beaten

¾ cup Cheddar cheese, shredded

1 T. butter or margarine, melted

¼ cup fine dry bread crumbs

Mix egg yolk, sour cream, and flour together; fold in beaten egg white. Layer ½ of the squash, ½ of the egg mixture, and ½ of the cheese in an 8x8 baking dish. Repeat layers; mix butter or margarine with crumbs and sprinkle atop. Bake at 350° for 20 minutes.

TOMATOES AND OKRA

1½ cups fresh okra, steamed until slightly
    tender

½ cup onion, chopped

¼ cup green pepper, chopped

2 T. oil

1 T. sugar

1 t. flour

½ t. salt

¼ t. pepper

2-3 tomatoes, peeled and quartered

Saute the onion and green pepper in the oil until tender. Blend in sugar, flour, salt and pepper. Add the tomatoes and heat through.

CHEEZY CAULIFLOWER

Break cauliflower into flowerettes. Steam until slightly tender. Place in 8x8 baking dish, sprinkle with salt. Combine ½ cup mayonnaise with 2 t. mustard; spread over the cauliflower. Top with 1 cup shredded sharp cheese. Bake at 375° for about 10 minutes, or until cheese is melted and bubbly.

BAKED CORN

1 egg, slightly beaten

$\frac{1}{3}$ cup evaporated milk

1 can (16 oz) cream-style corn

1 t. sugar

$\frac{1}{4}$ t. salt

$\frac{1}{4}$ cup green pepper, minced

1 T. pimento, chopped

1 T. onion, minced

Mix all ingredients together; cover with cracker crumbs and bake at 325° for 30-40 minutes.

DESSERTS

As far as I am concerned, the best desserts are pies. Yet, so many people shy away from making them because they feel incapable of making good pie crust. However, if you will follow the guidelines shown below and are willing to practice a little, you can become as good a pie maker as anyone!

PERFECT — FLAKY — PIECRUST

Single Crust Pie
1 cup flour
$\frac{1}{2}$ t. salt

Double Crust Pie
2 cups flour
1 t. salt

| ⅓ cup shortening | ⅔ cup shortening |
| 3 T. ice water | 6 T. ice water |

Step one: Combine flour (I prefer unbleached white) and salt. Blend the shortening into the flour evenly with a pastry blender until there is NO "flour powder" remaining in the bowl. This will assure you that the shortening has been blended in thoroughly with the flour.

Step two: Sprinkle the water over the flour mixture. With the back of a fork, push the dough from the outside of the bowl towards the center. Continue working in this manner until the dough begins to ball up in center of bowl.

Step three: Generously dust your hands and countertop with flour. Make a firm flat ball of the dough; do not work the dough any longer than necessary. Place on the floured countertop.

Step four: Dust rolling pin with flour; roll dough out by working in somewhat of an "X" motion. Occasionally pick up the dough and turn it a little. Add more flour to rolling pin, hands, or countertop as needed. Continue rolling the dough until you have a circular shape slightly larger than the pie plate.

Step five: Fold the dough in half and place in a greased 9-inch pie plate that has been dusted with flour. Open the fold to cover entire pie plate, being careful not to stretch the dough. Fit the dough comfortably to the contour of the pie plate avoiding air pockets.

Step six: For a single crust pie, trim the dough to ½ inch overhang. Turn the edges under to the rim of the pie plate and pinch the dough between your thumb and forefinger to form a fluted edge. For a double crust pie, use less overhang for both, about ⅛ to ¼ inch. Pinch the two edges together making sure they seal so fruit pies will not leak during baking. Fold edges under and flute as you would on the single crust pie; cut several slits on top crust.

Step seven: To bake a single crust baked pie shell, prick sides and bottom of dough with a fork at ½-inch intervals. Bake in a preheated oven at 450° for five minutes; check for air bubbles, prick more if needed. Continue baking an additional five or ten minutes until pie shell is golden brown. Place on a rack to cool.

MERINGUE
(For one 9-inch pie)

3 egg whites

½ t. vanilla

dash salt

5 T. sugar

Beat egg whites with salt and vanilla until soft peaks form. Gradually add sugar, beating until stiff and glossy peaks form and all sugar is dissolved. Spread meringue over hot filling, sealing to edges of pastry. Bake at 350° for 10-12 minutes or until meringue is slightly golden.

Additional Tips For Perfect Meringue:

- Separate eggs one at a time while still cold.

- For best volume, bring egg whites to room temperature before beating. If you are pressed for time, place the bowl containing the egg whites in another bowl containing an inch of warm water. Swirl egg whites occasionally with a spoon until they reach room temperature.

- Be certain beaters and bowl are completely clean and free of any trace of oil.

- Use a small deep bowl, preferably copper or stainless steel.

- After beating in sugar, test to see if all sugar is completely dissolved by rubbing a little meringue between thumb and forefinger. If it feels grainy, beat a little longer.

- Be sure meringue seals completely to rim of pie shell all the way around pie.

- Cool on a rack away from any drafts.

RETA'S CHOCOLATE MERINGUE PIE

1 cup sugar

4 T. flour

2 cups milk

3 egg yolks, slightly beaten with 1 T. water

2 oz. unsweetened baking chocolate

3 T. butter

1 T. vanilla

In saucepan, mix together sugar and flour; gradually add milk and stir well. Add egg yolks, chocolate squares, and butter. Cook and stir over medium heat until well blended and thickened. Remove from heat; add vanilla. Pour into baked pie shell. Top with meringue; bake at 350° 12-15 minutes or until golden brown.

CHOCOLATE ICEBOX PIE

1 baked pie shell

½ cup sugar

¼ cup cocoa

3 T. cornstarch

¼ t. salt

2 ½ cups milk

1½ t. vanilla

In saucepan, blend together sugar, cornstarch, cocoa, and salt. Gradually add the milk until well blended. Cook over medium heat and stir continuously until thickened and bubbly. Remove from heat and add vanilla. Cover filling with plastic wrap to prevent skin from forming on top. When filling has cooled some, pour into baked pie shell; again cover with plastic wrap. Place in refrigerator and chill thoroughly. Top with sweetened whipped cream and chocolate shavings. Keep refrigerated until ready to serve.

CUSTARD PIE

4 eggs

½ cup plus 2 T. sugar

½ t. salt

3 cups milk

1½ t. vanilla

¼ t. nutmeg

Beat eggs slightly in a large bowl; add sugar and salt; mix well. In a medium saucepan, heat milk to scalding or just below the boiling point. Gradually stir the hot milk into the egg mixture. Mix until well blended. Add vanilla and strain mixture into an unbaked pie shell. Sprinkle with nutmeg. Carefully place on lower shelf of oven and bake at 425° for 25 to 30 minutes.

PUMPKIN PIE

2 eggs, slightly beaten

1 can (16 oz) pumpkin

¾ cup sugar

¼ t. salt

1 t. cinnamon

¼ t. ginger

½ t. vanilla

1½ cups half & half

Combine all ingredients in order given; pour into 9-inch unbaked pie shell. Bake at 425° for 15 minutes. Reduce temperature to 350° and bake an additional 40 minutes or until knife inserted near center comes out clean. Cool and serve with sweetened whipped cream.

LEMON CAKE

1 box yellow cake mix

1 package (3 oz) lemon jello

4 eggs

2 t. lemon extract

¾ cup oil

Dissolve jello in 1 cup hot water; set aside. Mix eggs one at a time into the cake mix. Add the oil, lemon extract, and jello water. Beat until smooth; pour into greased and floured 9x13 inch baking pan. Bake at 350° for 25 minutes.

Glaze: Mix 1½ cups powdered sugar with ¼ cup lemon juice. Make holes in top of cake with a fork when you remove cake from oven. Pour glaze on cake while it is hot.

BAKED FUDGE

4 eggs, well beaten

2 cups sugar

4 T. cocoa

4 T. cornstarch

¼ t. salt

1 cup butter or margarine, melted

1 cup pecans, finely chopped

2 t. vanilla

½ cup heavy cream, whipped

Preheat oven to 325°. In medium bowl, beat eggs, sugar, cornstarch, cocoa, and salt until well blended. Stir in butter or margarine. Add pecans and vanilla. Pour mixture into 8x8 baking pan. Set pan in a 13x10-inch roasting pan. Pour boiling water into roasting pan to measure 1 inch. Bake for 45 minutes or until it is set like custard and crusty on top. Do not overbake. Remove from oven to wire rack. Let cool for 20 minutes; cut into squares. Serve with whipped cream.

COFFEE CAKE

1 package lemon cake mix

1 package (3 oz) lemon instant pudding

4 eggs

¾ cup oil

¾ cup water

Mix all ingredients together and beat well, about 8 minutes. Pour into greased 9x13 baking pan. Mix together:

1 cup sugar
1 T. cinnamon
½ cup nuts, chopped

Swirl on top of cake before baking. Bake at 350° about 45 minutes.

PANCAKES

1 cup white flour

½ cup whole wheat flour

3½ t. baking powder

2 t. sugar

½ t. salt

3 T. oil

1 egg, slightly beaten

1½ cups milk

In a medium bowl, mix together dry ingredients. In small bowl, combine egg, oil and milk; add to dry ingredients, stirring just till moistened. Bake on a hot griddle. Makes 6-8 pancakes.

Pecan Waffles: Make batter as directed for pancakes. Pour batter in waffle iron; sprinkle broken pecans atop waffle before baking.

GRANDMA'S WHOLE WHEAT BREAD

1 package active dry yeast

1 cup warm water

1 cup unbleached white flour

1 cup whole wheat flour (plus approximately ½-¾ cup to be added during kneading)

½ t. salt

2 T. oil

2 T. honey

In large bowl, soften yeast in warm water. Add remaining ingredients and stir with wooden spoon. Scrape out onto a well-floured surface. Have on hand additional whole wheat flour to keep hands dusted and to add to mixture as needed. Knead the dough for 8-10 minutes until it is smooth and satiny.* Place dough in a lightly greased bowl, turning once to grease surface. Cover with cloth and let rise in a warm place until double in size. Then punch dough down; be sure to push out any air pockets. Shape dough into a ball; cover and let rest 10 minutes. Shape into loaf and place in a greased bread pan. Let rise until double in size. Bake at 350° for 25-30 minutes. Rub top with margarine and cool on rack.

To Knead: Turn dough out on floured surface; curve fingers over dough and push down with heel of palm. Give dough a quarter turn; fold over and push down again. Repeat this method until dough is smooth and satiny.

BANANA NUT MUFFINS

⅓ cup shortening

⅔ cup sugar

2 eggs, slightly beaten

1¾ cup flour

3 t. baking powder

½ t. salt

3 medium bananas, mashed

2 t. vanilla

½ cup walnuts, broken into pieces

In large bowl, cream shortening with sugar until light and fluffy. Beat in eggs until mixture is thick and pale lemon colored. In small bowl, mix together flour, baking powder and salt. Blend into egg mixture alternately with bananas and vanilla. Mix in walnuts. Spoon batter into greased muffin pans. Bake at 350° for 20 minutes. Makes 12 muffins.

Oven Toast

Place buttered bread on the highest rack of oven at 425°. Bake until golden brown and toasty.

Cinnamon Toast: Sprinkle sugar and cinnamon atop buttered bread and bake as directed above.

Banana Toast: Add slices of bananas atop buttered bread; sprinkle generously with brown sugar.

The
Caterers
Can't
Always
Come

Entertaining

A Time to Share

Entertaining Tips

Table Settings

Menus for a Crowd

Other Great Recipes for a
Crowd

Romantic Dinners for Two

It was all there, like magic — the cake, the punch, the nuts, and oh, the food! I could hardly believe my eyes as I watched the well-dressed attendants take care of our guests. It was perfect! And when we came back later for pictures, the room was clean, with not a crumb to be found. This promised to be a wonderful life!

That was the wedding, but the servers and attendants didn't come home with us. However, we had loved the excitement of the crowd and enjoyed seeing their faces as they munched and talked. Through the years, Ed and I have continued to involve other people in our lives. We call it entertaining. And for most of us in those first years, the caterers can't always come.

After the wedding the rented crystal was gone, as was the lovely linen. But the most important ingredients for entertaining were present — the piano player and the barber.

In the pages that follow, you will find many ideas and menus for groups. Don't try to cook each recipe that I have offered; but look at this section as a growing one. You will have the rest of your lives to gather all the right serving pieces, and to learn how to arrange your guests. But, remember, the key is not to become intimidated just because the caterers didn't come home with you!

Entertaining ~
A Time to Share

Restaurants are nice, but they can be impersonal. Even the simplest meal in a home can be much more desirable. It took me a while to realize that fact, for I used to think that if everything were not perfect, there was little use in having company. But I was cheating my husband and myself out of an enriching experience to us through sharing our hospitality with others. Sharing even the simplest meal can be a lifeline to touching others.

My mother warned me years ago that if I waited to gain nice linens, beautiful dishes, crystal, a bigger home, or anything else before having friends over, I would be waiting for a long time; seldom in life is everything going to be that ideal! I began to make the most of what I had to work with and started to have dinners in my home. Of course, entertaining turned out to be great fun and satisfaction for all. Friendships don't depend on "things" at all.

Recently, I visited with a lady who shared her own experience with entertaining as a young wife. She had wanted to invite a group of couples over for a dinner party, but she did not have a large dining table or very many dishes. She solved the problem by borrowing card tables. Likewise, she borrowed dishes and tablewear from various individuals . Needless to say, she acquired a variety of colors and styles, so she established a color theme and mood for each table. The result was a beautiful dining room displaying a lovely array of colors and patterns. It was very effective, and it pleased her guests.

It is wise to select dinnerware within your price range. If you have chosen a very expensive pattern, it may take too many years and sacrifices to accumulate enough place settings to fit your needs.

Ed and I both have large families and most of them live in the same city that we live in. It is not uncommon for us to seat as many as 12 to 15 guests for a meal. For years, we only had one set of dishes, but we bought plenty of them; they were versatile and could be used both casually and more formally. Only recently have we been able to add a set specifically for formal dinners.

I know a woman who found that the pattern of her choice was being discontinued, so she was able to purchase many pieces at less than half price. She capitalized on the opportunity and ended up with all the specialty serving pieces as well as many place settings. Thus, she has had the enjoyment of a lovely and large set for many years, and without the usual cost! Where there is a will, there is a way!

A wonderful way to entertain guests when their number exceeds the capacity of your dining table is with a buffet. Whether formal or informal, buffet service is a delightful and flexible way to entertain. If you are not going to provide tables for seating the guests, be certain to serve foods that require a fork only. Once your dinner is prepared, relax! Enjoy your company by having your preparations done in advance. You need not overspend or try to do too much. Just a few personal touches contribute to style and make your guests feel special; that's what they'll remember the most.

Plan a menu with which you are comfortable and that has interesting and contrasting food colors and textures. Presentation is important; when food looks good, it seems to taste even better. Make one dish the main feature and let the others play a supportive role. Do everything you possibly can ahead of time. Take advantage of all preliminary steps in your recipes. If you are in the mood for a get together but have limited time, host a potluck dinner so friends can help. You might provide the meat dish and the beverages, and ask your guests to bring accompanying dishes and dessert.

However you choose to entertain, keep in mind what a treat it is to eat someone else's cooking. The meals that stand out most in my mind are not necessarily those that featured fancy dishes; but meals simply pulled together, sometimes with unplanned bits of this and that. They were born out of love and a desire to put our feet under the same table to share priceless moments of laughter and conversation.

Every season brings something to celebrate, along with various enjoyable customs and holidays. I encourage you to allow each season to inspire you with a harvest of new ideas. (For example, in the autumn, one friend uses large yellow leaves from her maple tree for place cards, writing names on them with a felt-tip pen.) Continue to develop your entertaining skills, and you will find many delicious ways to satisfy a wide variety of moods and occasions.

DUB'S BRIDGE

Here is a great party card game for a good-sized group. Set up card tables in various areas of your home.

1. No dummy, no bidding, no honors count.

2. Do not score as in bridge. Each trick counts 10.

3. Cut for deal each hand. Player on left of dealer leads.

4. Play partners. The side taking the most tricks is winner.

5. Keep your own score and take it with you.

6. Winners move after each hand is played.

7. Losers change partners.

NAME_____

SCORE

1. _____ Spades are trump.

2. _____ No trump. Winners add 100 to score.

3. _____ Clubs are trump. Winners and losers trade scores.

4. _____Hearts are trump. Do not look at hand. Play from table.

5. _____Spades are trump. Loser subtact 10 from score.

6. _____ Clubs are trump. Winner take all.

7. _____No trump. Winners add 200 to score.

8. _____ Diamonds are trump. Winners and
_____ losers trade scores.

9. _____Clubs are trump. Do not look at hand. Play from table.

10. _____Hearts are trump. Winners take all, UNLESS someone speaks while hand is being played — THEN other side takes all.

11. _____Cut for trump. Winners add 50 to score.

12. _____ No trump. Losers take all.

13. _____ Spades are trump. Losers subtract 10 from score.

14. _____Hearts are trump. Winners add 100 to score.

15. _____Spades are trump. Winners and losers trade scores.

16. _____No partners. Hearts are trump. Each player scores own tricks only.

17. _____ No trump. Each trick counts double.

TOTAL _____

~ Entertaining Tips ~

- The right mix of people can make or break your party. Invite both good listeners and good talkers. For formal occasions, mail the invitations. For casual ones, telephone friends approximately two weeks in advance.

- Keep an entertainment journal so you can remember which guests were present and what foods you served.

- Keep a record of close friends' and relatives' favorite dishes or desserts. When you honor them on a special occasion, you can prepare something they really like.

- Avoid a last-minute rush by setting your table well in advance; then cover it with a clean tablecloth until party time.

- Place appetizers and punches in different rooms so company won't crowd into one spot.

- Set out straight pretzel sticks instead of wooden picks for spearing meatball appetizers; you will not have to clean up any toothpicks.

- Add a festive flair to holiday plates by adding a few fresh cranberries next to sprigs of parsley.

- Use styrofoam egg cartons for ice trays when you need extra ice for entertaining.

- Mingle and enjoy your guests; learn to relax and leave most of the clean-up for later. Do *not* be picking up under your guests' feet.

- For plenty of ice on hand for a party, save and bag ice cubes a few days in advance.

- Invest in a large, 30-cup coffeemaker and a large tea urn. You need them for large groups.

- When serving buffet style, lay out your plates at the first of the line and your utensils at the end.

- For a change from the norm, host an elegant dessert buffet.

- Keep mulled cider or any warm party beverage hot by serving from a crock pot.

- For added flair in your punch bowl, use any metal mold and arrange slices of citrus fruits and maraschino cherries on the bottom. Fill the mold one-third full with fruit juice or water, and freeze. Then fill mold with additional juice or water and freeze until you are ready to use.

- Preserve cut flowers by adding two tablespoons of white vinegar and two tablespoons of sugar to one quart of water.

- For a pretty snowflake pattern on top of an unfrosted cake, place a paper doily on top and sift confectioner's sugar on top of the doily until all spaces are white. Lift carefully off the cake to reveal the pattern.

- Collect little baskets for serving breads, biscuits, and muffins.

- Flowers planted in a tube cake pan can make a colorful centerpiece for an outdoor umbrella table. Just insert the umbrella through the hole in the pan.

- For orange-peel curls, use a sharp knife and cut two, $\frac{1}{4}$-inch-wide strips through peel and membrane. Remove this layer of peel; separate into two strips. Twist each strip.

- Remnants from bolts of fabrics can be stitched into table coverings and matching napkins. Just measure and hemstitch the edges.

- A carved-out pumpkin serves nicely as a hearty autumn soup or stew bowl.

- To make chocolate leaves for garnish, brush melted semi-sweet chocolate with a small paint brush on the underside of non-toxic fresh leaves (lemon, mint, or ivy leaves). Chill on a baking sheet lined with waxed paper until hardened. Just before using, peel the fresh leaves away from the chocolate leaves.

- For decorative uses, brush clusters of grapes with slightly beaten egg white. Dip in granulated sugar and coating on all sides. Dry on a cake rack.

- To make apple rings, remove centers with apple corer. Slice apples crosswise into rings $\frac{1}{2}$-inch thick. Dip in lemon juice to retain color.

- To toast almonds, spread them on a cookie sheet and bake at 325° for about 15 minutes, stirring occasionally.

- To make carrot curls, use a potato peeler and cut thin lengthwise strips. Roll the strips up and secure with toothpicks. Chill in ice water until crisp and remove picks before serving.

- Have extra crushed ice on hand by storing water in milk cartons; freeze until needed, and slam carton on driveway to crush ice.

- When tossed salad makings have to wait, keep them fresh by covering them with paper towels wrung out in ice water.

- Candles burn more slowly and evenly if you place them in the freezer one hour before using.

~ *Table Settings* ~

BUFFET SETTING

One of the easiest ways of giving a party is the buffet. If possible, have tables set with flatware, napkins, and glasses. However, if these items are included on the serving table, place them last so the guest has one free hand as long as possible.

Guest lines should move from left to right. When serving soup, place at the end of the table to avoid spills, and serve in mugs for easy handling.

Dessert and coffee service should be set up in a separate location, or placed on serving table after the main courses have been removed.

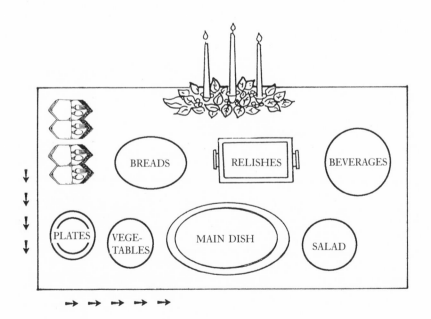

Sit Down Dinners

Sit down dinners can be either formal or informal; or they may include elements of each according to your needs. Plates should be 24 inches apart, and an inch from the edge of the table. Flatwear should be placed evenly from the outside toward the plate in the order of its use. The knife blades should face the plate. Beverages are always to the right of the water glass. Coffee cups are added later at the time of service.

Formal Place Setting

Informal Place Setting

Luncheon Place Setting

Napkin Folds

Fancy folded napkins add interest to your table. It is best to use large square cloth napkins that have been crisply starched to help keep the folds.

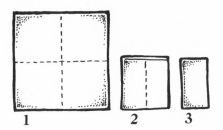

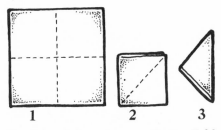

Traditional Dinner Fold

1. FOLD THE NAPKIN IN QUARTERS.
2. THEN FOLD IN HALF TO FORM A RECTANGLE.
3. PLACE THE OPEN EDGES NEXT TO THE FORK.

Traditional Luncheon or Buffet Fold

1. FOLD THE NAPKIN IN QUARTERS.
2. THEN FOLD IN HALF DIAGONALLY TO FORM A TRIANGLE.
3. PLACE FOLDED EDGE NEXT TO THE FORK.

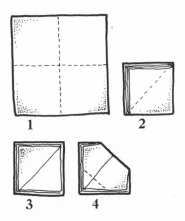

Buffet Server Fold

1. FOLD NAPKIN IN QUARTERS.
2. PLACE NAPKIN SO FREE POINTS ARE AT UPPER LEFT.

3. FOLD UPPER LEFT CORNER OF TOP LAYER DOWN TO LOWER RIGHT CORNER.
4. FOLD UNDER TOP RIGHT AND BOTTOM LEFT CORNERS.

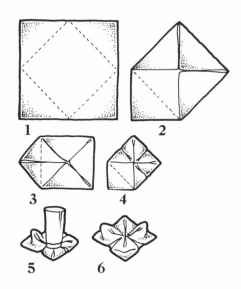

1. FOLD INTO TRIANGLE, CENTER POINT DOWN.
2. FOLD RIGHT AND LEFT POINTS TO CENTER POINT.
3. FOLD TOP CORNER DOWN TO ONE INCH ABOVE THE BOTTOM POINT.
4. TURN FOLDED POINT BACK TO UPPER EDGE.
5. TURN OVER. FOLD RIGHT AND LEFT POINTS ACROSS TO OVERLAP ONE INSIDE THE OTHER.

6. STAND AND TURN DOWN TWO UPPER CORNERS.

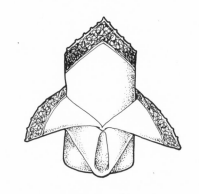

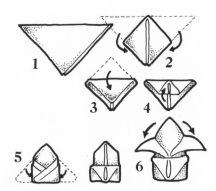

1. FOLD CORNERS OF NAPKIN TO CENTER.
2. NAPKIN WILL LOOK LIKE THIS WHEN ALL BUT LAST CORNER ARE FOLDED IN.
3. BRING THE NEW CORNERS TO THE CENTER.
4. TURN NAPKIN OVER AND FOLD CORNERS TO CENTER.
5. PLACE A GLASS IN CENTER OF NAPKIN TO ANCHOR IT. HOLD IT FIRMLY WITH ONE HAND AS YOU PULL OUT CORNERS FROM UNDERSIDE.
6. GIVE EACH CORNER A SLIGHT TUG TO MAKE IT STAND UP.

132

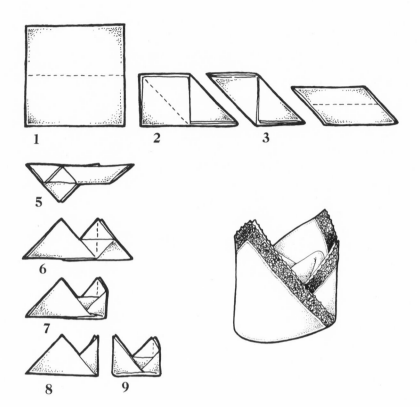

1. FOLD NAPKIN IN HALF TO MAKE A
   RECTANGLE.
2. FOLD TOP RIGHT CORNER DOWN
   TO BOTTOM EDGE.
3. FOLD BOTTOM LEFT CORNER UP
   TO TOP EDGE.
4. TURN NAPKIN OVER.
5. FOLD BOTTON EDGE UP TO TOP
   EDGE; ONE TRIANGLE WILL
   EXTEND BELOW BOTTOM EDGE.
6. HOLD NAPKIN ALONG TOP EDGE
   AS YOU TURN IT OVER. (A SECOND
   TRIANGLE WILL FALL FREE SO
   THERE WILL NOW BE TWO
   TRIANGLES ALONG THE TOP
   EDGE.)

7. FOLD RIGHT QUARTER OF THE
   NAPKIN TOWARD THE CENTER,
   TUCKING THE POINT UNDER THE
   LONG FOLD.
8. THE NAPKIN WILL LOOK LIKE
   THIS.
9. TURN NAPKIN OVER. ON THIS
   SIDE, FOLD RIGHT QUARTER
   TOWARD CENTER AND TUCK IN
   THE POINT. STAND NAPKIN UP.

~ *Menus for a Crowd* ~

MENU I

Chicken and Wild Rice Casserole
Spinach Salad
Deviled Eggs
Hot Bread
Iced Tea
Lemon Meringue Pie

CHICKEN/RICE

1 envelope (1⅜ oz.) dehydrated onion soup

2 cups sour cream

1 whole frying chicken (3-4 lbs.)

2 cups dry sherry

1 cup water

1 t. salt

1 t. pepper

½ t. basil

1 t. curry powder

7 T. parsley

1 can cream of mushroom soup

1½ cups uncooked wild rice

Mix onion soup into sour cream and allow to stand for 2 hours.
Place chicken in a dutch oven; pour sherry and water over it; add

seasonings and parsley. Cover and bake at 300° about one hour, or until tender. Remove chicken to cool; strain cooking juices into a saucepan and simmer until reduced to 1½ cups. Blend in soup; remove from heat and add sour cream mixture. Cook rice according to package directions. Bone the chicken and cut into small pieces; combine with cooked rice and turn into a buttered 9x13" casserole dish. Pour sauce over chicken and rice; toss slightly. Heat uncovered for 30 minutes at 250° in oven. (10 servings)

SPINACH SALAD

1 lb. fresh spinach

1 cup bean sprouts

small head of lettuce, chopped

1 cup sliced fresh mushrooms

6 slices of bacon (cooked and crumbled)

Carefully wash and drain spinach on paper towels; add other ingredients, toss lightly. When ready to serve, add dressing.

DRESSING

½ cup sugar

1 cup cooking oil

½ cup catsup

¼ cup vinegar

2 T. Worcestershire sauce

2 T. finely chopped onion

½ t. salt

LEMON MERINGUE PIE
(Makes 2, 9-inch pies)

3 cups sugar

¼ t. salt

⅔ cup plus 1 T. cornstarch

3 cups water

6 egg yolks, slightly beaten

2½ t. grated lemon rind

5 T. margarine or butter

⅓ cup fresh lemon juice

In a large, heavy-bottom saucepan, mix together sugar, salt and cornstarch. Slowly add water mixing well. Cook over medium heat, always stirring until mixture thickens and begins to boil. (It will become almost clear in color.) Allow mixture to boil 1-2 minutes or until thick while stirring. Remove from heat; add a small amount of hot mixture to the slightly beaten egg yolks, blending well; then return to the hot mixture. Bring to boiling again and stir for about two minutes longer. Remove from heat, add lemon rind and margarine. Very gradually add lemon juice.

Pour into 2 pre-baked (9-inch) pastry shells. Spread meringue on top, being certain to seal to the edge. Bake at 350° for 10-12 minutes. Cool away from drafts. Serve with hot coffee.

```
┌─────────────────────────────────────┐
│                                     │
│           MENU II                   │
│           ─────────                 │
│                                     │
│       Mexican Casserole             │
│         Avocado Salad               │
│         Tortilla Chips              │
│       Hot Buttered Bread            │
│        Iced Tea or Pop              │
│    Melt-In-Your-Mouth-Dessert       │
│                                     │
│                                     │
└─────────────────────────────────────┘
```

MEXICAN CASSEROLE

1 whole frying chicken (3 lbs.)

tortilla chips

1 cup chopped onion

⅔ cup chopped green pepper

1 t. chili powder

1 cup milk

1 can cream of chicken soup

1 can cream of mushroom soup

1 10-oz. can tomatoes and green chilies, chopped

8 oz. fresh mushrooms, thinly sliced

12 oz. sharp cheddar cheese, grated

Cover chicken with water in dutch oven; cover pan and simmer until very tender (about 1½ hours). Cool chicken, then bone and cube. Crush chips and spread in a 9x13 casserole dish; place chicken over chips. Blend all other ingredients except cheese, and pour over the chicken and chips. Bake uncovered at 350° for 20 minutes; add cheese and bake an additional 20 minutes. Remove from oven and let set for about 15 minutes. Serves 8.

Avocado Salad

    4 avocados

    4 T. (approx.) fresh lemon juice

    salt and pepper to taste

    4 medium tomatoes, chopped and drained

    lettuce

Mash avocados until smooth; gradually add lemon juice and beat until creamy. Add the salt and place mixture in a sealed glass jar to keep avocados from turning brown. At serving time, add tomatoes to the avocado mixture and arrange on lettuce leaves.

Melt-In-Your-Mouth Dessert

    1 cup melted margarine

    2 cups flour

    ½ cup chopped pecans

    8-oz. package cream cheese

    1 cup powdered sugar

    1 cup non-dairy whipped topping (Cool-Whip™)

    2 small packages *instant* pudding mix

    3 cups milk

    2 cups whipped topping (Cool-Whip™)

Combine the first 3 ingredients; press into 9x13 pan. Bake at 325° for about 15 minutes or until lightly browned; cool. Then combine the next 3 ingredients and blend until smooth. (The cream cheese needs to be room temperature.) Spread on top of the cooled bottom layer. Combine pudding mix with milk and follow package directions (using only 3 cups milk). Add atop cream cheese mixture. For final layer, top with about 2 more cups of Cool-Whip™; garnish with chocolate shavings. This dessert is much better if made a day in advance and allowed to chill thoroughly. Serves 15

MENU III

Spring/Summer Casserole
Cranberry Sauce Salad
Green Beans
Hot Rolls
Iced Tea or Punch
Coconut Cream Cake

SPRING/SUMMER CASSEROLE

3-4 cups cooked chicken, cubed

1½ cups chopped celery

⅔ cup chopped toasted almonds

1 t. salt

4 T. grated onion

1 cup mayonnaise

2 T. chopped pimento

4 T. fresh lemon juice

1 can cream of chicken soup

1½ cups grated Cheddar or American
   cheese

4 cups crushed potato chips

Combine all ingredients except cheese and chips. Toss lightly and spoon into large casserole dish. Spread cheese and chips on top. Bake at 350° for about 25 minutes or until heated and browned. Serves 8.

CRANBERRY SAUCE SALAD

2 packages (3 oz. each) raspberry jello

2 cups of hot water

1 can whole cranberry sauce (16 oz.)

1 cup chopped pecans

1 cup cold water

1 can crushed pineapple (20 oz.)

Dissolve gelatin in hot water; add cranberry sauce and stir until dissolved. Add cold water and crushed pineapple *with* juice. Add pecans. Chill until firmly set. Cut into squares and serve on lettuce leaf with a scoop of mayonnaise on top. Serves 12.

COCONUT CREAM CAKE

1¾ cup flaked coconut

2 cups sour cream

1¼ cup sugar

1 box yellow cake mix (18½ oz.)

8 oz. whipped topping (Cool-Whip™)

Mix coconut, sour cream, and sugar; chill overnight or six hours. Bake cake according to package directions in two round cake pans. Cool cake, then split each layer into two thin layers. Reserve 1¼ cups of the sour cream mixture; spread remaining mixture between cake layers. Mix the 1¼ reserved mixture with the whipped topping and frost the sides and top of cake. Seal in an airtight container and chill overnight. Serves 12.

MENU IV

Beef Stroganoff

Tossed Salad

Asparagus Tips

Hot Rolls

Iced Tea

Company Cheesecake

Coffee

BEEF STROGANOFF

2 lbs. beef sirloin, cut into ¼-in. strips

2 onions, chopped

½ cup margarine or cooking oil

2 cans of brown gravy or 2 envelopes gravy mix

1 lb. fresh mushrooms, sliced

8 T. butter or margarine

16-oz. package noodles

2 cups sour cream

In a large skillet, brown meat with onions in margarine or oil. Cover skillet and simmer until beef is tender, about $\frac{1}{2}$ hour. In saucepan, make gravy according to directions if using envelopes; or heat gravy if using canned. In a small skillet, cook mushrooms in 5 tablespoons of margarine or butter. Drain liquid from the beef; add mushrooms and gravy, heat thoroughly. Place noodles on a large platter; make a hole in the center of the noodles, add meat mixture to the hole; top with sour cream. Serves 6.

COMPANY CHEESECAKE

$1\frac{1}{2}$ cups graham-cracker crumbs

$\frac{1}{4}$ cup sugar

$\frac{1}{3}$ cup butter or margarine, melted

1 8 oz. package cream cheese

$\frac{1}{4}$ cup plus 1 t. sugar

1 egg, slightly beaten

2 t. vanilla

1 cup sour cream

1 T. sugar

1 can cherry pie filling

Mix together the graham cracker crumbs, $\frac{1}{4}$ cup sugar and $\frac{1}{3}$ cup melted butter or margarine. Press firmly into a 9-inch pie plate, bottom and sides.

Mix together cream cheese, $\frac{1}{4}$ cup plus 1 t. sugar with the egg and vanilla. Pour over the crust and bake at 350° for 20 minutes; cool completely.

Then mix together sour cream with 1 T. sugar and pour on top. Bake for 5 minutes at 425°. Cool and refrigerate. Add about half of the cherry pie filling for a topping. Keep chilled until serving time.

```
┌─────────────────────────────────────┐
│                                     │
│            MENU V                   │
│         ──────────                  │
│                                     │
│           Baked Ham                 │
│           Corn Soup                 │
│      Pineapple Cheese Dish          │
│          Green Beans                │
│           Hot Bread                 │
│            Iced Tea                 │
│           Pecan Pie                 │
│                                     │
└─────────────────────────────────────┘
```

BAKED HAM

You can use any good grade of ham. I like to use precooked ones, which of course doesn't mean you don't cook them some more. I especially like Hormel Cure 81™ hams. They come whole (about 8 lbs.) or you can buy them halved (3-4 lbs.) Unless you are having a lot of people for dinner, half a ham is plenty — it serves about 10. The Hormel Ham used to include a wonderful recipe for cranberry glaze, as follows:

> Combine 1 can of jellied cranberry sauce, 1 cup brown sugar, ¼ cup orange juice, ¼ teaspoon cinnamon, and ¼ teaspoon allspice. Heat slowly until smooth, beating with wire whisk. Spoon over ham the last ¼ hour of baking.

CORN SOUP

4 cups milk

2, 16-oz. cans cream stlye corn

1, 8-oz. can whole kernel corn, drained

3 egg yolks, slightly beaten

½ cup milk

¼ cup sugar

2 t. salt

3 T. flour

5 T. butter

¼ t. pepper

Combine the milk and corn in heavy saucepan and simmer for 15 minutes, stirring occasionally. Blend together the egg yolks, milk, sugar, salt and flour until smooth. Add a small amount of hot mixture to egg mixture and stir well. Gradually add egg mixture to hot mixture and simmer 20 more minutes. Add butter and pepper. Serves eight.

PINEAPPLE-CHEESE DISH

1, 20-oz. can pineapple chunks; drain and
    reserve juice

½ cup sugar

3 T. flour

1 cup grated cheddar cheese

¼ cup melted margarine

¼ cup Ritz cracker crumbs

Mix together all ingredients and place in greased one-quart dish. Bake at 350° until bubbly.

PECAN PIE

6 eggs, slightly beaten

1⅓ cups sugar

2 cups dark corn syrup

⅔ cup butter, melted

2 cups pecan halves

2 unbaked pastry shells (9 in.)

Mix eggs thoroughly with the sugar and a dash of salt. Add the corn syrup and gradually stir in the melted butter. Then add the pecans and pour mixture into the unbaked pastry shells, being careful that the pecans are equally distributed in both pies. Bake at 350° for 45-50 minutes or until knife inserted halfway between center and edge comes out clean. Cool and serve with a dollop of sweetened whipping cream.

```
┌─────────────────────────────────────┐
│                                     │
│             MENU VI                 │
│            ─────────                │
│                                     │
│           Brisket Roast             │
│           Garden Salad              │
│          Hominy Casserole           │
│            Hot Bread                │
│            Cold Drinks              │
│         Frozen Lemon Pie            │
│             Hot Coffee              │
│                                     │
└─────────────────────────────────────┘
```

BRISKET ROAST

Purchase a 3-4 lb. beef brisket. Place brisket with fat side up; pierce
with a fork, puncturing fat. Pour ¼ cup liquid smoke over top.
Wrap brisket, fat side still up, air-tight in aluminum foil and bake
very slowly in oven at 250° about 3½ - 4 hours. Remove from oven
and allow brisket to cool before slicing. Always slice the brisket
across the grain of the meat. Serve with a good barbecue sauce,
heated. Serves 8-10.

GARDEN SALAD

1 lb. fresh mushrooms, sliced

½ cup green onions, chopped

1 cucumber, peeled and sliced

¼ cup parsley, chopped

1 green pepper, thinly sliced

12 cherry tomatoes, halved

8 oz. swiss cheese, cut in thin strips

1 large can whole black olives, pitted

1 cup Italian dressing

Mix together all but the last ingredients in a large glass bowl. Place the olives on last and add dressing. Allow to marinate in refrigerator preferably overnight, but at least six hours. Add the cheese when you are ready to serve. Makes enough for eight servings.

HOMINY CASSEROLE

1 can cream of mushroom soup

4 green onions, chopped

6 oz. Cheese Whiz™ with jalapeña peppers

4 oz. Cheese Whiz™, regular

1 cup sour cream

2 cans yellow hominy, drained

⅓ cup crushed corn chips

Heat soup, green onions and cheese until melted together. Remove from heat and add the hominy and sour cream. Pour into buttered 8x8 casserole dish. Top with the corn chips and bake at 350° for about 20-25 minutes. This can be done somewhat ahead of time, for it is also good at room temperature. Serves 10.

FROZEN LEMON PIE

1 can (6 oz.) frozen lemonade concentrate

1 can Eagle™ brand milk

1 8 oz. container Cool Whip™

2 prebaked graham-cracker crusts (8 inch)

Mix together lemonade with the sweetened condensed milk. Fold in container of Cool Whip; squeeze in about ½ lemon. Place mixture into the graham-cracker shells and freeze. Tastes best if made a day or so in advance. Remove from freezer 10-15 minutes before serving.

MENU VII

Ladies' Luncheon

Tuna-Noodle Casserole
Lime Jello Salad
French Bread
Iced Tea
Amaw's Cherry Cobbler

TUNA-NOODLE CASSEROLE

1 package noodles, 8 oz.

1 can tuna, 9¼ oz., drained

⅔ cup mayonnaise

¾ cup celery, chopped

¼ cup onion, chopped

⅓ cup green pepper, chopped

¼ t. salt

½ t. pepper

1 can cream of celery soup

½ cup milk

1½ cups (6 oz.) sharp American cheese,
shredded

Cook noodles as directed on package. Meanwhile, mix the tuna and
mayonnaise together in a large mixing bowl. Saute the celery, onion
and green pepper in 2 T. of margarine until slightly tender; add to
tuna. In a saucepan, heat the soup with the milk, salt, and pepper.
Add cheese; when cheese melts, remove from heat. Drain the
noodles, fold into tuna mixture; stir in soup mixture; turn into a
casserole dish and bake uncovered at 400° for 20 minutes. Serves 8.

LIME JELLO SALAD

1 3-oz. package lime jello

1 small carton cottage cheese

1 cup crushed pineapple (drained)

1 cup whipping cream

1 cup boiling water

½ cup sugar

Dissolve jello in boiling water, add sugar. Whip; cool slightly; add
cream, whip again. Fold in cottage cheese and pineapple. Chill at
least 2-3 hours before serving. Serves 8-10.

AMAW'S CHERRY COBBLER

1 can cherry pie filling

1 can tart cherries, packed in water

¾ cup sugar

½ t. almond extract

2 T. butter

Mix all ingredients (except butter) together in a large bowl. Pour into buttered 9x13 baking dish; dot with butter. Prepare a single crust pastry recipe. Cut dough in strips about 1½ inches wide. Lay strips crosswise over cherry mixture. Sprinkle top with sugar. Bake at 400° about 35 minutes. Serve in dessert bowls with a dollop of whipped cream. Serves 8- 10.

MENU VIII

Weekend Brunch

Sausage-Egg Casserole
Mayme's Fruit Salad
Blueberry Buttermilk Muffins
Orange Juice/Coffee

SAUSAGE-EGG CASSEROLE

6 slices of bread, cubed

8 eggs

2 cups milk

1 t. salt

1 t. dry mustard

1 lb. sausage

1 cup grated cheddar cheese

Grease a 9x13 pan. Put bread on the bottom. In a bowl, beat eggs slightly. Add rest of ingredients except sausage. Cook and drain sausage and sprinkle over the bread. Pour on egg mixture; spread cheese on top. Refrigerate overnight or for 8 hours (covered). Bake uncovered in oven at 350° for about 30 minutes. Serves 8.

MAYME'S FRUIT SALAD

2 (1 lb. 14 oz.) cans apricots

3 (16 oz.) cans pineapple chunks

1 small jar maraschino cherries, drained

3 large bananas

1 (3 oz.) package vanilla pudding mix

2 T. sugar

1 T. butter or margarine

½ t. butter extract

Place fruit, except bananas, in a large bowl, reserving juice to make 2 cups. Cook pudding mix as directed, substituting the fruit juices for the milk and adding 2 T. sugar. When you remove pudding from the heat, add butter and butter extract. Cool and chill. Also chill fruit. Right before serving, cut up bananas and add to the bowl of fruit; then pour pudding mixture over the fruit and mix very gently. Serves 10-12.

BLUEBERRY BUTTERMILK MUFFINS

2 cups flour

½ cup whole wheat flour

1 cup sugar

¼ t. salt

1 cup buttermilk

2 eggs, slightly beaten

½ cup butter or margarine

½ cups fresh blueberries, rinsed and
drained (or dry-pack frozen ones)

Sift dry ingredients together in a large bowl. Make a well, add
buttermilk, eggs and butter which has been melted. Mix well; fold
in blueberries. Fill well-greased muffin tins about half full and bake
at 400° for 15-20 minutes. Serve warm. Makes about 2 dozen small
muffins.

~ Other Great Recipes For A Crowd ~

APPETIZERS AND HORS D' OEUVRES

CLAM DIP

1 6 oz. can minced clams

1 cup sour cream

1 T. minced onion, dry

½ t. salt

dash pepper

dash garlic powder

2 t. Worcestershire sauce

Drain clams; combine with other ingredients and chill. Serves four.

MEXICAN DIP

1 lb. hamburger meat, browned and drained

½ lb. sausage, bulk

1 small can refried beans

1 jar taco sauce (mild or hot)

2 lb. box Velveeta™ cheese, melted

Mix all ingredients together. Keep it warm and serve from a crock pot.

SAUSAGE BALLS

2 lbs. bulk sausage, 1 hot & 1 mild

3 cups Bisquick™

2 cups shredded cheddar cheese

Mix thoroughly and form into small balls. Place in greased pan and bake at 375° for about 15 minutes. Makes 90 balls.

HOT BEEF DIP

¼ cup chopped onion

2 T. margarine

1 8-oz. package cream cheese, cubed

1 cup milk

1 small jar dried beef, chopped

⅓ cup grated parmesan cheese

1 T. chopped parsley

Saute onion in margarine. Add cream cheese and milk. Stir over low heat until cream cheese is melted; stir in other ingredients and heat well. Serve hot with chips. Makes 2 cups.

PICANTE DIP

1 lb. Velveeta™ processed cheese spread, cubed

¼ cup milk

⅓ cup picante sauce

Combine all ingredients and heat over low heat until sauce is smooth. Serve with chips or raw vegetables. Makes 2½ cups

FRUIT PIZZA

Crust:

1 box yellow cake mix

4 T. brown sugar

4 T. water

4 T. margarine

2 eggs

1 t. almond flavoring

½ cup chopped pecans

Mix ½ of the cake mix with the brown sugar, water margarine, eggs, flavoring, and pecans. Then add the remaining cake mix; batter will be very thick. Spread on two well-greased 12-inch pizza pans. Bake 12 - 15 minutes at 350°. Cool about 5 minutes, loosen the crust and turn out on wire rack to cool completely; then returning to pizza pan.

Cream Topping:

1 package cream cheese (8 oz.)

1 cup powdered sugar

1 carton Cool Whip™ (12 oz.)

Spread cream topping on cooled crust. Top with fresh fruits of your choice such as: bananas, strawberries, grapes, kiwi, watermellon, cantaloupe, peaches, and pineapple.

MINIATURE PECAN TARTS

½ cup plus 1 T. margarine

3 oz. package cream cheese

1 cup flour

1 egg

¾ cup brown sugar

1 T. melted margarine

1 t. vanilla

⅔ cup chopped pecans

Bring cream cheese and margarine to room temperature; Stir in flour, blending well. Chill 1 hour and shape into 24 one-inch balls. Place each ball into tiny ungreased 1¾ inch muffin cups, pressing dough on bottom and sides of cups. Then, beat together egg, brown sugar, margarine, and vanilla until smooth. Add pecans and fill pastry lined cups with the mixture. Bake at 325° for 25 minutes. Cool and remove from pans.

LEMON BARS

1 cup margarine

2 cups flour

½ cup powdered sugar

4 eggs

2 cups sugar

4 T. flour

1 t. baking powder

4 T. lemon juice

Mix margarine in 9x13 cake pan. Mix the 2 cups of flour and powdered sugar; spread evenly over the melted margarine. Bake for 20 minutes at 350°.

Beat the eggs; add sugar, flour, baking powder and lemon juice; blend well. Pour onto hot crust and bake for 25 minutes at 350°. Sprinkle additional powdered sugar on top; cool 20 minutes and cut into bars.

HERB DIP

2 egg yolks

1½ T. lemon juice

½ t. dry mustard

dash of salt

⅔ cup olive oil

½ cup sour cream

1 T. fresh parsley, minced

1 t. fresh tarragon, minced

Combine egg yolks, lemon juice, dry mustard and salt. Beat together with electric mixer until thick and lemon colored. Gradually add oil, mixing just until well blended and thickened. Fold in remaining ingredients. Cover and chill. Makes one cup. Serve with fresh vegetables.

QUICKIE VEGETABLE DIP

Stir together one package of dry vegetable soup mix (1.4 oz.) with two cups of sour cream. Cover and refrigerate for 2 hours. Stir before serving.

CREAM CHEESE ROLLUPS

Simply spread softened cream cheese and chopped parsley on flour tortillas. Roll up like a jellyroll and cut into one-inch slices. Place a toothpick in each slice and serve with picante sauce.

TASTY HAM ROLLUPS

1 (8-oz.) package cream cheese

2 T. mayonnaise

2 t. Worcestershire sauce

1 t. instant minced onion

¼ t. dry mustard

dash of pepper

dash hot sauce

1-lb. package of thinly sliced ham

Combine all ingredients except ham, stirring until blended well. Spread mixture on each ham slice, roll up like a jellyroll and chill thoroughly. Shortly before serving, cut each roll into one-inch slices and arrange on a serving platter. Makes about 4 dozen slices.

BACON ROLL-UPS

2 (3-oz.) packages cream cheese, softened

½ jar chopped chives

1 t. milk

1 t. mayonnaise

25 slices of whole-wheat bread, cut in halves with crusts removed

25 slices of bacon, cut in half

½ t. garlic salt

Combine cheese, salt, milk, chives and mayonnaise. Spread each slice of bread with mixture and roll tightly. Wrap each roll with bacon and secure with toothpick. Bake at 350° for 30 minutes, turning occasionally.

SPINACH SQUARES

1 package (10 oz.) frozen spinach

1 can (14 oz.) artichoke hearts, drained and chopped

5 eggs

1 package cream cheese (8 oz.)

½ cup Parmesan cheese, grated

1 t. Italian seasoning

⅛ t. garlic powder

1 t. Worcestershire sauce

½ cup margarine, melted

½ cup onion, minced

¼ cup parsley, minced
1 cup Italian seasoned breadcrumbs

1 t. salt

½ t. pepper

Thaw spinach, drain well and squeeze dry. Blend eggs, cheeses, seasoning, garlic powder and Worcestershire sauce with mixer at medium speed. Fold in vegetables gently. Saute onion in the margarine, add to mixture along with the parsley, breadcrumbs, salt and pepper. Mix well and pour into buttered 8-inch square pan.

Bake 30 minutes at 325°. Cool completely, chill thoroughly and cut into squares. Makes 16 appetizers.

ARTICHOKE DIP

1 16 oz. can plain artichokes, drained and chopped

1 cup Parmesan cheese, grated

1 cup mayonnaise

Mix together and bake in lightly greased dish at 350° for 20 minutes. Serve hot with stoneground wheat crackers.

SPINACH DIP

1 package frozen chopped spinach (thaw and dry between paper towels)

½ cup parsley, chopped

½ cup green onion, chopped

1 cup sour cream

1 cup mayonnaise

1 t. Beaumonde seasoning

1 t. salt

1 t. lemon juice

1 t. dill seed

Mix and let set in refrigerator for several hours; serve with large corn chips.

BEVERAGES

SPICED TEA

1 stick cinnamon

2 cups pineapple juice

1½ cups orange juice

¾ cup lemon juice

1¼ cups sugar

4 cups water

Combine above ingredients and simmer for about 5 minutes; then add 3 quarts of strong tea. Serve hot. (Makes 6 quarts)

HOT CRANBERRY PUNCH

2 cups cranberry juice cocktail

2 cups pineapple juice

¼ cup water

¼ cup brown sugar

¼ T. whole cloves

½ T. whole allspice

4 sticks cinnamon, broken

Combine juices, water and brown sugar in large saucepan. Tie spices in coffee filter or square cloth and drop into liquid. Cover pan and heat until mixture comes to a boil. Reduce heat and simmer for five minutes. Remove bag of spices and keep mixture warm until serving time. This recipe can easily be doubled or tripled.

ORANGE SHERBET PUNCH

1 3-oz. package orange jello

1 12-oz. can frozen orange juice

1 46-oz. can pineapple juice

1 12-oz. can frozen lemonade

1 12-oz. can orange soda pop

½ gallon orange sherbet

Dissolve jello in 1 cup boiling water; then add 1 cup cold water. Add remaining ingredients except orange pop and sherbet, stirring well. Just before serving, add pop and sherbet cut into chunks.

SPICY APPLE CIDER DRINK

1 gallon apple cider

24 oz. ginger ale

4 cinnamon sticks

24 whole cloves

1 cup red hots

Pour cider and ginger ale into a 35-cup percolator. Place the cinnamon sticks, cloves, and red hots in the basket; perk as you would for coffee. Delicious and a great hot drink for Christmas Carolers!

EASY PUNCH

1 pkg. cherry Kool-aid™ mix

1 quart water

¾ cup sugar

1 6-oz. can frozen orange juice

1 bottle ginger ale (1 liter)

Mix all ingredients together except ginger ale; chill thoroughly. Just before serving, add ginger ale. Makes 15 servings.

ICED TEA

Heat 1 quart freshly drawn cold water to rolling boil; pour over one quart-size tea bag. Allow to steep 5 to 10 minutes, uncovered. Remove tea bag and tea is ready to serve when cooled. Serve in ice filled tea glasses; pass lemon slices and sugar.

NOTE: Keep tea at room temperature — refrigeration may cause cloudiness. If, however, tea does cloud, you can restore clear color by adding a small amount of boiling water.

MAMA'S HOT CHOCOLATE

1 T. cocoa

⅓ cup sugar

¼ cup water

3 cups milk

In heavy saucepan combine cocoa, sugar, and water. Bring to a boil and cook about 3 minutes. Gradually add milk; stir until heated thoroughly, never allowing the milk to come to a boil.

SALADS

MACARONI SALAD

1 small onion, chopped finely

2 green peppers, chopped

6 carrots, shredded

2 cups mayonnaise

¾ cup vinegar

1 can Eagle Brand™ milk

20-24 oz. macaroni, cooked

Toss together the onion, green peppers, and carrots; set aside. Combine mayonnaise, vinegar and condensed milk; add mixture to the vegetables; fold in macaroni. Chill thoroughly for 24 hours or keep on hand for as long as two weeks. Makes 16 servings.

POTATO SALAD

8 cups cooked potatoes, diced

4 hard-cooked eggs, chopped

2 cups chopped celery

½ cup onion, minced

¾ cup sweet pickle, chopped

3 t. salt

1 t. pepper

⅓ cup sugar

¼ cup vinegar

1¼ cups mayonnaise

Mix all ingredients; place in refrigerator and chill several hours before serving. Makes about 12 servings.

FROZEN PEA SALAD

2 (10-oz.) packages frozen peas

1 cup celery, chopped

6 green onions, chopped

¾ cup sour cream

¼ cup mayonnaise

1 t. Beaumonde spice

¼ lb. bacon, cooked crisp and crumbled

1 cup Spanish peanuts

Mix all ingredients together except peanuts. Add the nuts just before serving.

CHERRY SALAD

1 can cherry pie filling

1 can Eagle brand condensed milk

1 (8 oz.) carton Cool Whip™

1 can (16 oz.) crushed pineapple, drained

½ cup pecans, chopped

Blend together all ingredients and keep chilled. Delicious!

SIDE DISHES

PARTY POTATOES

32 oz. frozen hash brown potatoes

1 t. salt

½ t. pepper

1 can cream of chicken soup

½ cup chopped onion

1½ cups sour cream

2 cups grated cheddar cheese

2 cups corn flakes cereal, crushed

¼ cup margarine, melted

Mix together the first 7 ingredients. Place in a greased 9x13 baking pan. Cover with the cereal and margarine mixture; bake at 350° for about an hour. Serves 8.

BROCCOLI RICE CASSEROLE

½ cup margarine

1 package (10 oz.) chopped frozen broccoli

1 onion, chopped

1 can cream of chicken soup

½ cup Cheese Whiz™

½ cup milk

1½ cups minute rice

Blend well and remove from heat. Cook rice according to package directions; add to broccoli mixture. Pour into buttered casserole dish and bake at 350° 20-30 minutes. Serves 8.

MACARONI AND CHEESE

2 cups cooked macaroni

½ onion, chopped

1 cup mayonnaise

1 jar sliced mushrooms, 3-4 oz. jar of pimentos

1 can cream of mushroom soup

1 lb. Velveeta cheese

2 cups corn flakes, crushed

Mix all ingredients together except the corn flakes. Place in a buttered casserole dish; top with the corn flakes and bake at 350° for 30 minutes. Serves 8.

SCALLOPED POTATOES

4 cups milk

2 eggs

2 t. salt

1 t. black pepper

8 T. margarine, melted

4 lbs. potatoes

½ cup onion, chopped

2 T. margarine

½ cup dry bread crumbs

In large bowl, blend together milk, egg, salt and pepper. Saute onions until tender in 2 T. of margarine and set aside. Peel the potatoes and cut into thin slices. Coat a very large baking dish with the melted margarine. Arrange a layer of potatoes in bottom of baking dish and top with onions. Cover with half of one the egg mixtures. Repeat layers again, dot with margarine; sprinkle top with crumbs and bake covered for 45 minutes at 350°. Remove cover and continue cooking until lightly browned. Serves 12.

MAIN DISHES

CHICKEN-BROCCOLI CASSEROLE

1 (3-4 lb.) fryer (cooked, boned and cubed)

1 can cream of chicken soup

1 package (10 oz.) frozen chopped
broccoli, thawed

1 cup celery, chopped

1 onion, chopped

1 jar (8 oz.) Cheez Whiz™

1 package (8 oz.) Minute Rice™

1½ cups potato chips, crushed

Cook rice as directed on package. Fold Cheez Whiz into rice; mix in other ingredients. Pour in a 9x13 baking dish and bake for one hour at 350°. Serves 8.

Chicken and Spaghetti Dinner

1 large fryer (cooked, boned, and cubed)

1 7-oz. package of spaghetti

1 onion, chopped

1 green pepper, chopped

1 can cream of mushroom soup

1 can cream of chicken soup

1 cup milk

½ t. garlic salt

1 t. chili powder

½ lb. American cheese, grated

Cook spaghetti in chicken broth and drain. In a large saucepan, saute onion and green pepper in a little margarine. Add soups, milk, and seasonings. Fold in chicken and spaghetti; simmer 10 minutes. Pour into a greased casserole dish and sprinkle with cheese. Bake at 350° for 30-40 minutes.

Spinach Lasagna

1 lb. ground chuck

1 lb. ground pork

2 envelopes spaghetti sauce mix

2 T. instant minced onion

1 t. garlic salt

1 t. salt

1 large can Italian tomatoes (28 oz.)

1 package (10 oz.) frozen spinach

2 eggs

2 cups cottage cheese, cream style

¾ cup Parmesan cheese, grated

1 package (16 oz.) lasagna noodles

1 package (8 oz.) Swiss cheese

Brown the meat in large skillet; drain. Stir in spaghetti sauce mix, onion, garlic salt and tomatoes. Simmer, stirring often, for 5 minutes. Remove from heat. Cook spinach and drain very well. Beat eggs and stir in cottage cheese, Parmesan cheese and spinach. Cook noodles according to package directions, drain and cool. Lightly grease a baking dish (9x13) and spoon in just enough sauce to cover bottom. Layer ⅓ of the noodles and ⅓ of the cheese mixture; repeat to make 2 more layers of each. Cut the Swiss cheese into strips and arrange on top. Bake at 350° for 30 minutes or until bubbly. Makes 8 servings.

DESSERTS

BUTTERMILK BROWNIES

2 cups flour

2 cups sugar

1 cup margarine

4 T. cocoa

1 cup water

½ cup buttermilk

2 eggs, slightly beaten

1 t. baking soda

1 t. cinnamon

1 t. vanilla

½ t. red food color

In large mixing bowl, stir together the flour and sugar. In a saucepan, mix the margarine, cocoa and water together and bring to a rapid boil. Pour hot mixture over the flour and sugar stirring well. Add buttermilk, eggs, soda, cinnamon, vanilla and food coloring. Mix well and pour into greased pan (15½x10½x1 inch). Bake at 400° 12 to 15 minutes.

Five minutes before brownies are baked, begin preparing frosting; spread on while brownies are still hot.

FROSTING

¼ cup margarine

4 T. cocoa

6 T. milk

1 box powered sugar

1 t. vanilla

½ cup pecans, chopped

½ Correction ½ c. margarine

In saucepan, mix margarine, cocoa, and milk together; bring to boiling. Remove from heat and add powdered sugar, vanilla and nuts. Beat well and spread on brownies immediately. Cool; cut into bars.

SUPREME PINEAPPLE CAKE

1 pkg. yellow cake mix

1 can (14 oz) crushed pineapple

1 cup sugar

1 large package vanilla pudding mix

1 carton (8 oz) Cool Whip™

¼ cup flaked coconut

Bake cake in 9x13 pan as directed on package; let cool. In saucepan, combine pineapple with juice and sugar. Bring to a boil and stir until sugar is dissolved.

Poke holes in the cake with a fork and spread pineapple mixture over the cake.

Prepare the pudding as directed on box; cool slightly; top cake with pudding. Cover cake with foil and refrigerate overnight.

Before serving, spread Cool Whip on the top and sprinkle with the coconut. Makes a very rich and lucious dessert!

STRAWBERRY CAKE

1 pkg. white cake mix

3 T. flour

1 (3 oz) box strawberry jello

½ cup water

¾ cup cooking oil

4 eggs

½ cup frozen strawberries, thawed

Mix all ingredients except the strawberries. Beat until smooth; add berries, beat one more minute. Pour into 2 greased and floured 8-inch cake pans. Bake at 350° 30-40 minutes. Let cool and frost.

FROSTING

½ cup margarine

1 box powdered sugar

½ t. salt

½ cup strawberries

Cream margarine, sugar and salt together. Add thawed berries and beat well. Spread between layers and on top and sides.

PISTACHIO CAKE

¼ cup sugar

½ cup nuts, finely chopped

1 t. cinnamon

1 package yellow cake mix

1 small package pistachio instant pudding
   mix

4 eggs

½ cup sour cream

¼ cup oil

¾ t. almond extract

5 drops green food coloring

Combine sugar, nuts and cinnamon; set aside. Combine remaining ingredients in large mixing bowl. Beat at medium speed for 4 minutes. Pour ⅓ of the batter into greased and floured 10-inch tube pan; sprinkle with half the sugar mixture. Repeat layers and top with remaining batter. Bake at 350° for 45 to 50 minutes. Cool in pan for about 15 minutes. Remove and finish cooling on rack. If desired, drizzle with powdered sugar frosting. (Much like a coffee cake — very good.)

CELEBRATION BANANA CAKE

¾ cup shortenting   ½ t. salt

1½ cups sugar   1 t. soda

2 eggs	½ cup buttermilk
1 cup bananas, mashed	1 t. vanilla
1¾ cups flour	½ cup pecans, chopped
1 t. baking powder	1 cup flaked coconut

Cream shortening and sugar until fluffy. Add eggs; beat 2 minutes at medium speed. Add bananas and beat 2 minutes. Add blended dry ingredients alternately with buttermilk and vanilla; beat 2 more minutes. Stir in pecans. Pour into two greased and floured 9-inch round pans. Sprinkle ½ cup coconut on each layer. Bake at 375° for 25-30 minutes. Remove from pans and cool, coconut side up, on racks. Place first layer, coconut side down, on cake plate and spread on Creamy Nut Filling. Add second layer, coconut side up. Swirl Snow frosting around sides and about 1 inch around top edge, leaving center top unfrosted.

CREAMY NUT FILLING

½ cup sugar	½ cup chopped pecans
2 T. flour	¼ t. salt
½ cup cream	1 t. vanilla
2 T. margarine	

Combine first 4 ingredients in saucepan. Cook over medium heat until thickened. Add pecans, salt, and vanilla; cool. Spread between cake layers.

SNOW FROSTING

1 egg white	½ t. vanilla
¼ cup shortening	½ t. coconut extract
¼ cup margarine	2 cups powdered sugar

Cream together the first 5 ingredients until well blended. Add sugar, beating until fluffy. Spread on cake.

BANANA ICE CREAM

6 cups milk

9 egg yolks, slightly beaten

1¾ cups sugar

½ t. salt

3 cups half and half cream

2 T. vanilla

4-5 bananas, mashed

Mix sugar, salt and egg yolks. Pour on milk and cook in a very havy saucepan over medium heat. Cook until sugar is dissolved and egg yolks are done, never allowing mixture to boil. Cool, strain, add cream and vanilla. Fold in mashed bananas. Pour into chilled can of ice cream maker, being sure not to overfill. Place dasher in can and place lid on firmly.

Mix one part rock salt with eight parts chrushed ice. Fill ice cream freezer tub with this mixture well above the line of the mix in the cream container. Turn crank, slowly increasing speed as the mixture begins to freeze. (If using electric freezer, simply plug in unit.) To complete freezing process, drain off brine and pack tub with a mixture of 3 parts ice to 1 part rock salt. Let stand for at least 30 minutes before serving. Makes about 12 servings.

~ *Romantic Dinners for Two* ~

Entertaining is a great way to be with close friends, and gives the opportunity to make new friends. It is an enjoyable and satisfying way to extend your hospitality to others you care for very much.

But the sweetest, most important entertaining you do will be the private moments you create to be alone with your husband — intimate little dinners for two! It is the perfect way to keep the romance in your relationship, and provides a time to reflect the sheer joy of being in love; a time for renewal and refreshment as a couple.

I encourage you to periodically turn routine meals into special events and celebrations. Set the table with your prettiest dinnerware, bring in fresh flowers, add soft music, and dim the lights. Arrange a unique and beautiful evening that reminds you both how special you are to one another — an evening that focuses on nothing else but your love, and gives you precious moments to cherish always.

```
┌─────────────────────────────────────┐
│                                     │
│           MENU I                    │
│           ──────                    │
│                                     │
│       Cornish Hens with Rice        │
│          Waldorf Salad              │
│        Buttered Asparagus           │
│         Hot Bread Sticks            │
│          Apricot Cake               │
│            Coffee                   │
│                                     │
└─────────────────────────────────────┘
```

CORNISH HENS WITH RICE

2, 1-pound Cornish game hens

salt

pepper

Preheat oven to 350°. Remove giblets from hens and season inside and out with salt and pepper. Place hens breast side up on rack in shallow roasting pan. Brush with melted butter; place pan on lower position of oven, and roast uncovered for 1¼ to 1½ hours. During roasting, baste frequently with additional melted butter. NOTE: If hens brown too quickly, place foil loosely over top of hens.

CHEDDAR CHEESE RICE

Cook ½ cup uncooked long-grain rice according to package directions. Add ⅓ can cream of mushroom soup, 1 egg yolk (slightly beaten), 1 tablespoon diced pimento, ⅓ cup shredded Cheddar cheese, salt and pepper to taste. Spoon mixture into a small casserole dish greased lightly. Bake at 350° for 25 minutes. Garnish with parsley.

WALDORF SALAD

2 apples, coarsely chopped

2 stalks celery, chopped

1 can (8¼ oz.) pineapple chunks, drained

½ cup mayonnaise

½ cup nuts, chopped

Toss all ingredients. Serve on salad greens if desired.

APRICOT CAKE

1 can (21 oz.) apricot pie filling

1 package white cake mix, *one-layer size*

1 egg

⅓ cup pecans, chopped

½ cup flaked coconut

½ cup butter, melted

Spread pie filling in bottom of square baking dish. Combine cake mix, ⅓ cup of water and egg. Beat several minutes at medium speed with electric mixer. Pour over pie filling; sprinkle with pecans and coconut. Drizzle butter on top and bake in oven at 350° for 35 minutes. Serve warm; add a dollop of whipped cream on top if desired.

```
┌─────────────────────────────────┐
│                                 │
│          MENU II                │
│         ─────────               │
│                                 │
│    Stuffed Chicken Breasts      │
│      Cranberry Delight          │
│     Sweet Potatoes Supreme      │
│    Green Beans — Hot Rolls      │
│  Ice Cream with Chocolate Sauce │
│      Iced Tea  Coffee           │
│                                 │
└─────────────────────────────────┘
```

STUFFED CHICKEN BREASTS

2 large chicken breast halves, skinned and deboned

2 T. chopped onion

¼ cup chopped green pepper

1 small clove garlic, minced

3 T. margarine, melted

¼ cup herb-seasoning stuffing mix

⅓ cup water

¼ t. salt

¼ t. pepper

3 T. margarine

¼ can cream of chicken soup

1 T. dry white wine

2 T. herb-seasoned stuffing mix

Place chicken between 2 sheets of waxed paper; flatten to ¼ inch thickness with a rolling pin or heavy object. Saute onion, green pepper, and garlic in 3 T. of margarine. Stir in stuffing mix and the water, salt, and pepper. Spread mixture evenly on the chicken breasts; fold short ends of chicken over stuffing; roll up and secure with wooden picks. Brown chicken in 3 T. of margarine and place in small baking dish. Combine soup and wine; pour over chicken. Sprinkle with 1 T. herb stuffing mix. Cover with foil and bake at 325° for 45 minutes.

CRANBERRY DELIGHT

1 package (3 oz.) raspberry jello

1 cup boiling water

½ cup cold water

⅔ cup Mandarin orange segments, drained

1 can (8¼ oz.) crushed pineapple, drained

1 can (16 oz.) whole cranberry sauce

2 T. chopped pecans

* * *

mayonnaise for topping

grapes for garnish

Dissolve jello in boiling water; add cold water and chill until partially set. Stir in orange segments, pineapple, cranberry sauce, and pecans. Spoon mixture into 8x8 inch dish or into individual molds. Chill until firm. Top with a dollop of mayonnaise and garnish with frosted grapes.

FROSTED GRAPES

Dip grapes into slightly beaten egg white; then dip into granulated sugar. Place on waxed paper and refrigerate several hours.

Sweet Potatoes Supreme

1½ cups cooked sweet potatoes

1 t. vanilla

¼ cup margarine, melted

1 egg

½ cup sugar

In mixing bowl, add potatoes, egg and beat well; add vanilla, margarine, and sugar; beat again. Place into a buttered casserole dish. Sprinkle with topping and bake 20 minutes at 350°.

Topping

½ cup brown sugar

2½ T. flour

½ cup chopped pecans

2 T. margarine

Blend with pastry blender until crumbly.

Ice cream with Chocolate Sauce

¼ cup sugar

1½ T. cornstarch

⅛ t. salt

2 T. cocoa

1 ¼ cups milk

1 t. vanilla

In a small saucepan, blend sugar, cornstarch, salt, and cocoa; add milk gradually. Cook and stir over medium heat until thickened and bubbly. Remove from heat and cover with plastic wrap to prevent skin from forming on top of sauce. Cool completely. At serving time, place one scoop of vanilla ice cream in bottom of wine glass, followed by a scoop of chocolate sauce. Repeat for another layer; garnish with a dollop of whipped cream and chocolate shavings.

MENU III

Saucy Pork Chops
Deviled Eggs
Marinated Green Beans
Twice Baked Potatoes
Brown 'n Serve Rolls
Lemon-Topped Cake
Coffee

SAUCY PORK CHOPS

2 loin pork chops, ¾ inch thick

½ onion, sliced

1 green pepper, cored and sliced

1 can (8 oz.) tomato sauce

¼ t. salt

⅛ t. pepper

Brown pork chops slowly in a small amount of oil; drain off any excess oil. Add onion and green pepper on top. Pour on tomato sauce and add seasonings. Cover and simmer slowly for about 45 minutes or until the chops are very tender.

Deviled Eggs

2 hard-cooked eggs

1½ T. mayonnaise

¼ t. mustard

salt and pepper to taste

Cut peeled eggs lengthwise into halves. Slip out yolks; mash with fork. Mix in mayonnaise, mustard, salt, and pepper. Fill whites with egg yolk mixture. Cover and refrigerate until thoroughly chilled.

Marinated Green Beans

¼ cup sour cream

2 T. Italian salad dressing

1 can (8 oz.) cut green beans, drained

1 tomato, peeled, cubed, and drained

1 T. onion, finely chopped

Combine sour cream and dressing. Add beans, tomato, and onion; mix well. Chill several hours; serve in lettuce cups.

Twice-Baked Potatoes

Scrub 2 baking potatoes and rub with shortening for softer skins. Prick with fork to allow steam to escape. Bake until tender at 350° for about 1¼ hours. Cut thin lengthwise slice from each potato;

scoop out inside, leaving a thin shell. Mash potatoes until no lumps remain. Beat in about ¼ cup of milk and 1 T. margarine, salt, and pepper. Beat vigorously unitl fluffy.

Fill potato with mixture; sprinkle with shredded cheese. Place on ungreased cookie sheet and bake at 400° for about 20 minutes, or until filling is golden brown.

LEMON-TOPPED CAKE

1 store-bought angel food cake

* * * *

¼ cup sugar

2 t. cornstarch

dash of salt

dash of nutmeg

½ cup cold water

1 egg yolk, beaten

1 T. margarine

¼ t. grated lemon peel

1 T. lemon juice

In small saucepan, combine first 4 ingredients. Stir in water and cook over low heat until mixture thickens and bubbles. Stir small amount of hot mixture into the beaten yolk; return to hot mixture; cook and stir one minute longer. Remove from heat and add margarine, lemon peel and lemon juice, blending thoroughly. Serve over slices of angel cake.

SALMON PATTIES

1 (8-oz.) can salmon, drained and flaked; bones removed

½ cup crackers, crushed

1 T. onion, minced

1 egg, slightly beaten

1 T. lemon juice

1 T. celery, minced

¼ t. salt

⅛ t. pepper

Mix all ingredients together; form into patties and brown slowly in a small amount of oil until golden brown and heated throughout. Serve with creamy dill sauce:

DILL SAUCE

1 T. margarine

2 T. flour

¼ t. salt

⅛ t. pepper

1 cup milk

1 t. snipped dill weed, or ½ t. dried dill
weed

dash of nutmeg

Heat margarine in a small saucepan over low heat. Stir in flour,
salt, and pepper. Cook until mixture is smooth and bubbly; remove
from heat and stir in milk. Return to heat and cook one more
minute. Remove from heat and add dill weed and nutmeg.

SPINACH QUICHE

1 cup chicken broth

1 8-oz. container cream-style cottage cheese

1 large egg

1 package (10 oz.) frozen chopped spinach,
thawed and *well drained*

⅔ cup shredded Swiss cheese

1 T. grated Parmesan cheese

⅛ t. ground nutmeg

dash pepper

Blend together broth, cottage cheese and egg in a covered blender
until smooth. In a large bowl, combine remaining ingredients. Stir

in broth mixture. Pour into greased 8-inch pie pan and bake at 350°
for 40 minutes or until set.

HERB ROLLS

Cut hard rolls in halves; spread with a mixture of ¼ cup butter, 1
teaspoon minced green onion, 1 teaspoon minced parsley and
¼ teaspoon dried rosemary. Wrap rolls in foil and heat at 350° for
10-12 minutes.

LEMON PUDDING CAKE

1 egg, separated
⅓ cup milk
½ t. lemon peel, grated
2½ T. lemon juice
½ cup sugar
2 T. flour
dash of salt

Heat oven to 350°. Beat egg white until stiff peaks form; set aside.
Beat egg yolk slightly, add milk, lemon peel, and lemon juice; add
sugar, flour, and salt, beating until smooth. Fold into egg white and
pour into a small ungreased casserole dish. Place dish in a square
8x8 inch pan on oven rack; pour very hot water into pan to 1 inch in
depth. Bake until brown, about 30 - 35 minutes. Remove casserole
dish from water.

. . . wishing you a happy home and a happy marriage — may your home be a place of peace and your love a continued strength.

General Index

Index of Recipes

~ *About the Author* ~

Curly reddish-brown hair, a face that smiles from the heart, petite, independent and determined are but a few of the characteristics and qualities that describe the author, Sharon Collins.

After 31 years of shared life with Ed, Sharon unselfishly shares with the new bride straightforward and realistic information as well as insights and encouragements that are so important to the bride as she bravely, and many times blindly, steps into an exciting world of challenges after the wedding.

Sharon and Ed Collins share their lives together in Tulsa, Oklahoma, along with their three adult children, Lisa, Paul and Valerie and their two granddaughters, Sarah and Kora.

A graduate of The University of Tulsa with a degree in music, Sharon teaches piano in her own studio and is the staff pianist for her church.